Doul...

"We'd have a shamrock-green iced cake for St Patrick's day, one with daffodil-yellow icing to celebrate Easter, but best of all we loved Your Ma's Christmas cakes."

Noa (Finola) is one of a family of nine children ("double the boys to girls") growing up in Northern Ireland and she tells of their squabbles and adventures together with humour and affection.

Michelle Carrington

Other autobiographies and stories of family history in Lions and Tracks

Private, Keep Out *Gwen Grant*
Isaac Campion *Janni Howker*
When Hitler Stole Pink Rabbit *Judith Kerr*
Harold and Bella, Jammy and Me *Robert Leeson*
The Fib and Other Stories *George Layton*
The Girls in the Velvet Frame *Adèle Geras*
Poona Company *Farrukh Dhondy*
Granny was a Buffer Girl *Berlie Doherty*
A Sound of Chariots *Mollie Hunter*

Finola Sumner

Double the Boys

Illustrated by Martin Salisbury

First published in Great Britain in Lions 1990

Lions is an imprint of
the Children's Division, part of
the Collins Publishing Group,
8 Grafton Street, London W1X 3LA

Copyright © Finola Sumner 1990
Illustrations copyright © Martin Salisbury 1990
All rights reserved

Conditions of Sale
This book is sold subject to the condition
that it shall not, by way of trade or otherwise,
be lent, re-sold, hired out or otherwise circulated
without the publisher's prior consent in any form of
binding or cover other than that in which it is
published and without a similar condition
including this condition being imposed
on the subsequent purchaser

1

Our family never seemed to me to be quite ordinary. There were nine of us children for a start, and double the boys to girls. There wasn't much over a year or so in age between us all and not much in appearance either. Officially the fairer, freckled-face side favoured our mother, and the paler, darker our father, but what with the lot of us having the same regular-enough features, eyes more or less blue, give or take the freckles, and a dimple or two, you had us all.

It wasn't the nine children. In itself, that was nothing to write home about, hovering not much above average, I suppose, for Ireland in those days, North or South. It was in other ways that it struck you. There were the names. We often accused our mother of having found them in her older prayer book. We'd have been outcasts, laughed off the street with the half of them, if our brother Joe the eldest boy – and normally named – had not been something of a leader out there. Not that it would really have mattered. We children had our own street gang made. It was a family they faced.

Joe was a big strapping boy, tall for his age, and he did a lot of thinking. He didn't so much inspire as order us around in a very officer-like way. He was keen on the army and had a lot of old army books. He had been very keen on cowboys before that. He was the first in our town – so far as we knew – to have actually sent away to Hollywood for a big signed photo of the Lone Star Ranger and his horse. He had found the form on the back of an American comic.

The day the photo arrived we were all very impressed. Our doorbell never stopped as children came in their legions to see for themselves Miss Joe's Yank photograph. All the boys in our family were called "Miss". Whether it was a childhood try to equal the sexes or our mother's forlorn hope of making the boys gentler, it stuck. Down the line from Miss Joe came Miss Kilian, Miss Sean, Miss Malachy, Miss Connor and Declan the family baby. We even at one stage had Miss Mammy, and Miss Daddy, but in the course of time as we grew older and wiser, they got promoted to "Your Ma" and "Your Da".

Our house lay slap in the middle of a street which had the town's two main schools at either end of it. From our front door, up the street to the left was the Convent Girls, to the right the Abbey Boys, run by an order of Christian Brothers. So we found ourselves in the thick of it almost the whole day long, as processions of uniformed boys going one way, girls the other, passed by. In time our house found its true role as a halfway stage where greetings could be exchanged, meetings arranged, and plans explained, all under the guise of seeing if one of us was coming out to play.

Miss Mammy our mother must have been a remarkable woman to keep order at all in such a big mob of children. She was a great storyteller and could turn her hand to almost anything. She had wanted to become a teacher, but in the ways of those days had been taken from her training and sent first out to America to help one emigrant brother start up there, then back to help another start up at home, where she'd met and married our Da. Perhaps we were lucky it turned out that way, though as children we would sigh and moan.

"Oh, Miss Mammy, how could you have come back to this here old North? Just think," we'd cry, "we could be living away over there in Yankeeland, lying on them there beaches, chewing all that there bubble gum. Why, you might even have married a cowboy."

So we'd tease and sigh our Yankee dreams and she would smile and say, "These things are meant to be and turn out for the best in the long run." This in time was to become her motto.

Miss Kilian, the second eldest boy, started out family life called "Big Head", which was a fact. "It's all them brains in there, packed with promise," our aunt did say about him. This was proved true, for in time he cleverly twisted the name to suit himself. First the "Big" was dropped and for a while he was known as "Head", then by some further manoeuvring

"Head" became "King", finally immortalized as "the King".

Our doorbell would ring and some small schoolboy would be found standing there. "The King's forgotten his football boots, I'm just here to fetch them," he'd say in a rush. Of an evening it would be, "The King's forgotten his surplice". By then Kilian was an altar boy, soon to be head altar boy, long since a professor.

Next in the line-up was Miss Sean. He was quiet and clever and maths was his subject. In many ways he had too fine a mind for the rough and tumble of our family, but as he slept in Joe's room he became his trusted lieutenant. He had fame as well from his ability to do his sums well. This talent was called upon endlessly.

"Now figure me this one out," the old folk would say.

"Miss Sean, will you help me with this here wild stupid sum?" would be more our line.

Then came Malachy, "Miss Malachy". He had a sweet smile and was perhaps the best athlete of the boys, though that was ever hotly disputed. He was easily the best-tempered.

Miss Connor came after and being quite young was but a junior family member. One above the other, that's how it was. Declan, the last boy, never had a courtesy title at all. He was christened "Babynun" right from the start, being the last of the boys to attend the mixed Infants School run by the nuns on the hill.

Young as he was, Babynun was everybody's message boy, even then putting in the footwork for his

future career in accountancy. "Babynun, will you go and fetch my Latin book from upstairs?" – "Babynun, will you run and buy me a toffee apple?" – "Babynun, will you dash up the street and tell me friend, Your Ma says, I'm not allowed out to play." – "How much?" he'd say. In time he grew rich, even Your Ma borrowed from him.

The eldest girl, Miss Eilish, was known as the Boss. She was a good cook and tennis-player and, much better still, a great spinner of yarns and dreams. Being the oldest of all and often put in charge, this ability was brought early to the fore.

"Now," she'd say to us, "pay heed: if you clean your shoes for tomorrow, tidy your rooms, finish your homework, find Your Ma's lost pinking scissors . . . when you've completed all that and everything is as clean as a new pin, you're to go to the backyard – that by the way's to be like a new pin as well – then each of you is to draw with this here chalk a circle, and in the circle stand. Shut tight your eyes, turn three times and wish, only one wish, mark you, and it will come true."

"When?" we'd cry.

"On the very same moment," she'd reply. By such methods did she keep authority.

There we'd stand in the now clean-as-a-new-pin backyard each in our magic circles, wishing our hearts out. Those wishes never came true, but there was always a reason. "Call them there shoes clean!" she'd cry. "That room tidy! Sure, those aren't the right scissors anyhow. You'll just have to try harder next time." Even Joe joined in the wishing game. He used to wish to be let run away to join the cowboys. I wished for sweets, sweets galore for ever more.

Miss Bronagh, the youngest girl, was the only one of us to have actually seen Santa Claus. Your Ma had hidden her under the tea table one Christmas Eve when she'd been unable to sleep and gone downstairs about it, and he'd called. She charged a penny for a full recount of it all.

And then there was me, Miss Noa, the middle girl between Miss Eilish and Miss Bronagh – third from the top of the whole family or sixth from the bottom depending on which way you'd care to approach it. I was often a thousand miles away it seems, though in and out of everything and every bit as bad as the rest; a born fidget. My own fame lay like St Anthony's in my knack of finding lost things. I can still hear the calls, "Miss Noa, you're to come in quick. Your Ma's lost her darning needle, Babynun's dummytit, the vanilla essence for her sponge, the safety pins." Whatever it was, I had the patience to look and knew whom to petition up above. "Oh good St Anthony, Patron and Finder of Lost Things, please help me in this my quest." There was nothing to it once you'd learnt your lines.

On the subject of Miss Connor and Babynun's pram-walk after school I was the one least vocal. Your Ma would have them ready and waiting when school was over. You handed in your satchel and got them in return. I didn't mind at all. I would sing them lullabies, and pretend the whole while they were just a pair of wee dolls.

Your Da was a powerful man. He had his own

hackney-cab business. He had himself been the youngest of six brothers in his own family. "A mixed bunch," he said of them, "aye, went down the hill badly. Sure, they owned half the town till they let it slip." He'd stop to shake his head slowly, the pipe always in the mouth. "The cabs, the cars they had, the God's amount of money they went through." Now himself down to a cab or two but his own, the nature of his business kept him in touch with all the comings and goings of the town. Not much passed Your Da's eyes. He hadn't had much of an education but was a born leader, and reckoned a holy terror when you did wrong. Nobody, but nobody, answered back Your Da. First there'd be his famous glare of a look, then the roar. Under it, though, he had a heart of pure gold and a great sense of humour. He could shake with great laughter for minutes at a time, the pipe dangling dangerously from the mouth. When he was good and ready, he'd give his big smile. "Sure, you don't know the half of it."

He was a firm believer in the best: "Aim ever for it, keep far away from the trash." In this Your Ma and he were in accord. "Here today, gone tomorrow, flibberty-gibbets, never lasted."

Your Da was always on the go. If he had no fares, he'd leave the carstands where the town's cabs parked, and come back home to start on his heart's work – his building! We had a bit of land to our house with a lock of old tumbledown sheds in that. Here he would dream of having a big working garage one day, and the furtherance of his building career.

Your Ma sighed, having lived through his earlier

efforts. He had already rebuilt the bathroom, the scullery, constructed a very odd-shaped outdoor laundry complete with mangle, while she worked on round him. When Your Da was in a building mood anything could happen. Then he'd be forever tapping on walls. "Just testing its value," he called it. You never knew when you came home from school which bit of the house would be gone next. "It went up in a cloud of smoke," Your Ma reported. To give him his due, when the job was complete, mostly it was better than new.

Your Da loved employing workmen on his building efforts and he'd tell them what to do. In he'd come of an evening, dressed in his good dark suit, fill the pipe with tobacco, stand back and survey.

"Jimmy, you appear to be a sensible man, but that's not going to work at all, there's no purchase there. Have ye a minute, wait till I show you how to lay them yokes right," he'd say to the town's best plumber. "Mick, the very man I want to see: I believe I've got the measure of this wall at last," he'd instruct the specialist bricky. It wouldn't be long, suiting action to words, till he took matters into his own hands. "Shore it up here, coax it out there, easy now, nice and slowly does it," and dismantling half the day's work at one go. They didn't say much, usually nodded only, "Aye . . . wouldn't go the whole way with you, maybe you've something there though," as they watched the pride of their achievement more or less undone. Even they treated Your Da carefully.

We girls got off lightly, considering, but each boy in turn was summoned from his books or his play to give a hand's turn on the new working garage. They often worked late into the night.

"They'll founder themselves," Your Ma often cried.

"None the worse for it, it'll knock the steam out of them," Your Da simply replied.

Finally she put her foot down about their studies. A good education had to take priority. *"There was no stake in else."* Your Da agreed in his way but he couldn't be deprived of lieutenants. If no workmen showed up he sent for his sons. Your Da needed an audience. His own recipe for happiness was to have all his sons in place and himself in charge. Although he wasn't adverse to lashing out with the weight of his hand when he let rip; they had a few rough moments in their lives, looking back.

Strangely, Your Da was a soft touch for all the odd bodies around, not to mention his great weakness for the Yanks. He'd give the time of day to any of them. Your Ma never knew whom he might turn up with next – returning members of families, remembered, if at all, only in prayer, itinerant folk with wandering memories, tipsy farmers who'd mislaid their horse and cart out of town, travelling clergy waiting for trains, a Yank of any degree, to-ing and fro-ing, intent on his roots. She lived through them all.

His favourite odd body though was one he christened "Fortescue". To my mother he was more woebegone and dirtier than a tinkerman, but Your Da often brought him home to lunch, Fortescue riding in style in the big black cab. He'd shuffle in, his best hobnail boots stuffed with newspaper, an old rope tied round his middle, and would puff on a queer-smelling chalk pipe.

"A shower of blessings on ye, woman of the house," he saluted my mother. The boys' Latin master, a student of these matters, said this salutation was a fine example of direct translation from the Gaelic.

Fortescue then sat down by the fire and spoke to no one but my Da. "A true knight of the road, that man sitting there," Your Da told us. "He has travelled the length and breadth of Ireland. Ah, many's a tale he keeps under his hat, isn't that right, Fortescue?" and Fortescue would nod. "He never had a chance," my Da went on. "Now if he'd only got himself to Americay, he'd have been a different man. More power to his elbow was all he needed. By the powers, Fortescue, there'd have been no stopping you then. The Yanks are the people! Put that in your pipe and smoke it," he informed the whole wide-eyed audience of us. He said things like that, Your Da.

Perhaps it was because his own family had run out of steam early that Your Da had a natural sympathy with such odd fellows. For before "the slip", we'd been told, his had been a family of some note in the town, descended from the old horsedrawn carriage trade, and all deadly handsome, it appeared, into the bargain. They'd let it all slip due to the horses and the drink. Hard workers, good fighters, they'd started off, ending only in heavy-gambling, big-drinking men, now scattered to the four corners of the earth. In fact, as we charted it back, it would appear that Your Ma's main marriage vows for Your Da, or what he'd laid down for himself, were the same: for him to take the pledge, and never so much as look at a racehorse again. Thus he wore for ever more a shiny Pioneer pin, the teetotaller's pledge, on his lapel, moving it from suit to suit as he changed them. It was no small achievement for a man who went, in the course of his business, almost daily to weddings. He usually drove the bride.

When Your Da was on a wedding that was great steam. We'd fight to clean out whichever taxi cab he had used, collecting the confetti and rose petals. He always brought home for Your Ma the little piece of wedding cake he'd been given, all wrapped up in a white lacy paper doily. At grander dos, it came in a wee silver box, often with a charm of a horseshoe attached. Your Ma became quite an expert: "It could have done with a shade more raisins or currants," she'd pronounce. "I wouldn't give you two pins for the marzipan. I'd have given it a tint less almond myself," she'd conclude, while making it into nine token pieces as best she could, so we'd all have a bit to make a wish.

To Your Da the dividing line between the right-reared families and not was bought chips. He took the lowest view of them. We were not allowed them, full stop. "Brought up on chips" was his favourite insult. He often referred to people as nothing but a crowd of chipheads. "There goes Hunger's Mother who feeds her children on chips," he'd say of some poor woman or other. The way we children saw it, they were born lucky who had bought chips for their supper.

As Your Da kept his own timing because of his job, he wasn't always in place at the same time of an evening. But you'd soon know he'd arrived. You could tell by the fire, he was such a holy terror for minding it. In he'd come, the fire flaming happily away, at peace in its grate, but for Your Da it was never enough. He attacked it, and stacked it, rebuilding its shape, adding logs all the while, as it spat back at him in vain in his face. "Just building its body up", he called it.

"Holy Mother of God, you'll set the chimney on fire," Your Ma always cried at length as the flames roared higher and higher and well out of their grate. He often did, but sadly for us he was his own Fire Brigade. If it got truly out of hand, he'd hose it himself, swinging one of the big hoses he used for washing the cars round from the garage.

You'd call upstairs to anyone missing.

"Miss Joe, Miss Connor, Babynun, come quick, Your Da's fire's on fire again," so nobody would miss the sport. The boiler attached would register complaint and rumble all evening.

"It's overheating itself, I am sure," implored Your Ma.

"Ah, it'll be as right as rain when a few of them have a bath or two," answered back Your Da.

You might be sent to have two or three of an evening, to relieve the hot water. But Your Da never learned to stop playing with the fire. He had great stacks of pokers and tongs for his game. And last thing at night he'd slack it all down to keep it in play for the morning.

Our mother was a very holy woman and kind in every way. She cycled to Mass almost every day of the year, rising up early for the first one just after six. That, so she said, gave her hope for the day, those few moments of peace and quiet over her breakfast were worth every ha'pence before we descended for school to drive her astray.

This routine was shattered daily in Lent when we all had to go. There were two churches in the town: Your Ma's favourite was the smaller one, the furthest away, but it had the earlier Mass. The big cathedral was nearer, but kept later hours.

We'd set off on our bicycles in different directions, each trying to get there first so as to get the best seat for getting out fast. We'd position ourselves strategically round the little church, which was only full of mothers and old women that early, our eyes fixed on one another. After Communion, when you'd been to the altar, taking slanty looks at each other, all hell broke loose. First one of us didn't go back to the right seat, but would flit back a few rows. The next one, seeing this, did just the same, and on down the line a perpetual changing of places began. The idea of it was to see who'd get nearest the door. Old women looked up first in fear, then in anger, their prayers disturbed by "yet another of them fidgety children" on the move again. The point of it all was that who ever did get out fast could grab their bike, and be home first to get to the toaster.

Your Ma often looked round, catching sight of a whole row of us kneeling in that very back pew, waiting for those last words of release, "The Mass is ended. Go in peace. Thanks be to God." She'd shake her head at us threateningly.

Back home, the familiar morning chorus began. "Who's taken me school bag?" – "I've lost all my homework." – "The cat's been at me Latin." Your Da wisely slept late to avoid this barrage.

As we lived in the same street as the school, we came back home for lunch.

"In no time at all," my mother did say, "sure, I've only seen the last of you out and the first one is back." But, with a patience born of prayer, maybe, she had a big hot lunch ready for us, and, run off her feet like she was, the same at evening time too. We were a two-dinner family.

The door would burst open and in we'd come, often with a few friends from the country smuggled in alongside, those ones who normally ate sandwiches or bought sweets. Then, like there was no tomorrow, the clamour began. I can hear it now: "I really can't wait, I have to be gone in a minute, a moment, a second." – "My friend is tired waiting out there." The bell never ceased. Someone would run to attend it.

"Is Bronagh coming out?"

'No.'

"Tell her hello, then."

"Is Malachy ready yet?"

"No."

"Tell him goodbye then."

"The King can't come home, so Your Ma's to send him up something . . . I'm just here to fetch it."

Delegations coming and going the whole while, messages left, sacred secrets told, thin plots thickened up, all in the space of under an hour. It's no wonder our mother said we'd drive her to the mad house or the poorhouse, depending on whether her nerves or finances were uppermost that day. Either way you look at it, it seems a great wonder now she wasn't driven astray.

2

In the evenings, we went back on the street to play with the other children, often gathering round the old gas lamplight. The boys would be doing handstands, playing with catapults, conkers, marbles, chasing moths, throwing shadows, whatever was in season. We girls swung on a rope from the lamp-post before the lamp men came to make us take it down, then it was back to hopscotch or "wee house". "Wee house" involved brushing every single speck of dust in a space to make dust walls for the shapes of rooms and doors. Then you could go visiting each other's wee dust house.

The familiar street cries of our family would ring out. How long ago it seems now; it makes you smile.

"Miss Joe, you're to come in, for saying a curse."

"Miss Kilian, you're for it. You stuck out your tongue and called some poor squinty wee child Glassy

Two Eyes. You were heard, Your Ma says, with her own ears from inside."

"Tell-tale tattle. Buy a penny rattle."

"You snake in the grass."

The street was one big play yard those days. Safe as houses, it was. Any "bad elements", as your elders did call them, doubtless bored, usually left and joined the town's Corner Boys. Their corners were down the main street of town where the bright lights were. "On the road to ruin. Be singing for pennies in no time with their uneven ways," was said of them. Many of them, champion whistlers, you'd hear them while passing on your way to and from Mass, as they grouped in their corners, not possessive of space, which was just as well, for our family often acted as if it owned the whole street. Miss Sean and Mis Malachy took over most of it, chalking out white tram lines just about everywhere. The pair of them then hammered big blocks of firewood together with a lock of rusty old nails. They'd have quite a few carriages attached and tin-tops from bottles for wheels. Then down on their hunkers, happy as larks, they went "chuff-chuffing" for hours. People sidestepped so as not to walk in them. They had the street in their keeping well into the summer and they got very vexed if a real jalopy were to use it. We girls of the street had to fight for some space to chalk out our hopscotch. These lines lasted way into the summer too.

One of our favourite plans for the street was to open a wee shop from our house on to it.

Miss Eilish was the worst at it. "Why can I not turn this here room into a nice wee shop?" she would beg of Your Ma. "Sure, you only use it at Christmas. Your Da could knock a hole through there in no time."

Your Ma's face was a picture, knowing full well Your Da was perfectly capable of doing just that to her best front room with all her carefully put-away ornaments, precious treasures, some from her time in America.

All was as nothing beside Miss Eilish's dream of her shop. "But what can we use for the answer?" she always cried in conclusion. That was her name for the counter.

Your Ma finally gave her for her "answer" a few rickety old wooden orange crates which Miss Eilish put across the front door. These she spread with old newspapers, held in place by a stone. Her candy apples were a great success. They were finished off with a slim ice-cream slider wafer on top. They had a strange shape, but quite a few school children passing by homeward did buy them.

Soon "Wee Shops" operating from front doors spread like wildfire up and down the street, opening only at home time for the schools. But such is fashion, I suppose, that they didn't last, and pocket money returned to the real shops, the ones with the hard black and white sandwich toffee bars.

The main street games followed the church year and were seasonal in kind if oddly entwined. Starting off in Lent, we all went off sweets, but none of us refused any in the offing. Instead, we collected them like marbles or stamps.

On a Lenten evening we would sit beneath the old street gas-lamp, our sweet collections stored in cardboard shoeboxes proudly before us. Children from so far as a dozen streets away arrived with their collections which were fingered, appraised, and if a deal was struck, swapped.

A hard toffee bar of liquorice with the white sandwich middle was highly prized, worth more than its weight in chocolate or ordinary gum. A screw of real American bubblegum was a prize to end all. You had a straight swap of anything and the pick of a few single sweets of any sort for it. Scrupulous we were about not breaking our fast, spitting conscientiously on our hands after handling the sweets, in case a lick found its way on to the tip of our tongues by mistake. By the time Lent was over, those sweets were past their best, and in a sad sorry mess.

Floppy toffee bars of the softer variety, now stretched bandy beyond repair, jelly babies missing their heads, lollipops bereft of their sticks, anything that had got itself too dusted in sherbet or fluff, all now could be had for one single sweet in a wrapper. After the Lent sweet trade, the glossy newness of the next morning's Easter egg was a sight to behold.

After Mass on Easter morning, we collected in our street to show our eggs off to each other. They came in every sort and size. Girls had ones in pretty straw baskets, the eggs big or small, one or two, maybe a few, depending on style, nestling in the coloured straw. Each basket was daintily held over the arm so as to give it more care.

Boys usually had theirs in boxes and were very self-conscious about carrying them at all. Not many Easter eggs came wrapped in tinselly paper then, most came as they were, or at the most in glassy paper, still displaying right off the rich glossy dark of the chocolate, often embroidered with palely iced flowers.

We could judge at a glance, old hands at it, which were filled with sweets, which sadly hollow, and which heavy with a thick cream filling. Most of us were reluctant to break them open at all. An aura of privacy somehow surrounded Easter eggs. Rarely, even behind the scenes, were bits of them traded.

3

In no time came summer, when we went out in relays to stay in the country with Cissie Dash, so named for being always in a hurry. Cissie was but a cousin of our mother's, but to everyone of us, in due course, was to become more than a most special aunt.

Her husband Matt was a steady farmer, and did what he was told. He said very little, usually, "Ahem, certainly so", to just about everythng. They had no children of their own.

"Cissie could have run an empire single-handed," Your Da said of her. She was a tiny slip of a woman but chock-full of energy.

"She'd knock spots off the lot of us put together," was Your Ma's comment.

Cissie had quite a superior farm with a lot of land to it, and a lovely old farmhouse covered in roses. There was nothing she wouldn't give a chance to. She had fancy hens who got sickly, turkeys and geese, horses and cows, pigs, goats, a donkey who ran with the cows to eat certain weeds, and honey bees. She also kept the service bull for the townland but we girls never saw much of that side of things. What with blackbirds and thrushes singing, donkeys braying, and cocks crowing from dawn, it was a hive of activity and music the whole day long.

Cissie Dash, the power behind the throne, had a passion for work,

"Be her own death one of these days," people said in wonder of her.

Interested in everything, new or old, she was famous for the great spread she put on her table. That woman could rise with the rooster, have milked half the cows, have the windfall apples collected up in her apron, have the big oaken table all set, and be churning fresh butter by the time we awoke to the smell of newly baked bread.

"Sure the morning's half-gone," she'd cry by eight o'clock or so, cooking great goose-egg omelettes with rashers of bacon for breakfast and fetching warm milk from the first cow to drink with it. How much was combined in one person.

As a relic from the old hiring fairs, many of the big farms those days had a changing number of farm hands who came and went with the seasons. They arrived from all over, from as far away as the South or as near as the local orphanage. Cissie, with her spirit of giving all creatures a chance, had a succession of some very odd ones pass through her farm before they were given their walking papers, even from her.

But she kept the same two live-in lads for the land

the whole year long. They came and went too, but they mostly were there. We got to know them well as Micky and Pat.

Micky cut quite a dash with his thick wavy hair. He hailed from a family with a big farm down in the South, but spoke of them little. You got the feeling there was no love lost there now. A lad with a ready twinkle in his eye and a lilt to his voice, we girls supposed he looked all right, though he fancied himself. Joe thought him a big blather, a real flash, while Cissie found him a rip of a boy at the best of times but a steady worker withall, it seemed.

"No better man to have round a farm. Had horse sense, knew his oats." Matt vouched for him.

Pat was altogether different, being from the orphanage and one for the prayers. The two of them got on together well enough, each having what the other was wanting. Pat loaned the money to Micky for his dances, Micky paid him back by taking him along. Lacking the gumption, dance halls were the last place Pat would have gone on his own.

"I'm afraid one of life's tulips, the lad," was how Micky saw it.

At dusk of an evening they'd meet up with the lads from neighbouring farms at one or other's crossroads. They came by bike, often using the crossroads by Cissie's; Micky had constructed a den there which he christened "The Shanty". Here by candlelight they whiled away the hours, gambling at cards, sharing out their smokes, and slugging between them a bottle of the hard stuff just down from the hills.

Cissie and Matt wore the pledge, though they

minded little what other souls did, if the work didn't suffer and those in their care showed a rosy appetite ever, and didn't rust at their food. They partook of the sacraments in rotation and were seen in the church when required.

On a still summer's evening with not a stir in the air, the lads, having abandoned their den, would sit dilly-dallying outside on the ditch by the leafy crossroads, and survey any passing traffic and the lie of the land. A gaggle of us girls from around, hiding in the hawthorn hege, spent hour after hour spying on them. The stories they told under those trees! We'd long given up blushing to the roots at them.

Mostly they were to do with Micky's lovelorn affairs. He had his eye on a silver-service waitress in the main street hotel in the town as we all knew. But it seemed there was competition from the chef, too. The other lads were forever pulling his leg about her.

" 'Tis what I'd call a pretty thing," Micky would sigh in his broad brogue. "Oh the wiggle of her, she has me destroyed," he'd moan. "Do you know what she said?"

"What?"

"She'd never met the likes of me before. See, there you have it."

"You big dolt."

"Oh, isn't it dandy? A little bird told me she's cracked about me. You wait, I'll have her in the double seat at the pictures, if not up the creek next. Man alive, we'll click yet. There's a good time coming, oh doodah, doodah, dey."

Under pretext of looking for a runaway cow or a

hen, in a tangle of green, we'd creep out of the hawthorn hedge in the end and be seen. There'd be a dead hush.

"Well, me darlings, show us your dimples then," this from Micky, the others joining in with great giddy yahoos. By now we were a heap of shy giggles.

"I suppose one of ye wouldn't want a wee court?" this again from Micky. "Well, run away on then before the bogey man gets you."

You couldn't see us for dust, though as we grew older we stood our ground, and codded them back. In one way and another we learnt quite lot from them, I suppose.

On a Saturday evening, Micky and Pat got ready for the big dance in town, the hooley, they called it, and the weekly "wee court". We watched as they shaved with an old cut-throat blade, sharpening it first on a long leather thong. When they were decked out in their good Sunday suits, we helped with their tie-pins and the wave in their hair, settling the cows-lick they'd already oiled in. Micky would be giving a running commentary the whole while on who he was going to give "the wee court" to that night in the town, if the silver-service waitress wasn't around. Or he'd be humming "Old Smokey", a song he made very much his own.

In high heart, they snapped the bicycle clips to their legs and were ready for off, amid warnings from Cissie when to come back and how to behave. Like a motherly hen she spun them round for inspection, maybe restraightening a tie-pin we girls had attended to. Then she slipped some money into their breast pockets. They never seemed to get wages as such, but a good home with their keep, and what she felt fit found its way there on a Saturday night. In a jaunty mood they pedalled off, Micky on his low-handled racer, Pat on his rusty old bike which was always slipping its chain or breaking a spoke.

Sunday morning Cissie dug them out of bed, sleepy-eyed, for the last Mass. "It's like waking the dead," she'd cry – the last thing they needed, both fagged out but they knew they hadn't a ghost of a chance. They'd settle in back to work on a Monday morning, often joining happily for a day or two in our games. We argued the toss, time after time, on whose chosen hens laid the most eggs. You could depend on Micky to remove a good dozen from some other henhouse to yours if you were in favour. His favour was provisional on the loan of an ear to his bragging of the past Saturday's clicks in the town. He spared little detail. We reckoned among ourselves that he made the half of it up and had definitely a slate loose in his head.

When the big turf fire was lit, brightly sparkling in the inner room, and the oil lamp settled, Cissie and Matt sat down to take their heart's ease after the work of the day. It wasn't long though till some other body appeared.

"Who darkens the door?" Cissie called out, on hearing, she thought, a footfall without, but more often than not someone just appeared in your midst. Not many knocked, but they simply lifted the latch and made their way in. If you left the room for a tick, your chair could be gone. "Some poor oul soul," as Cissie said of them, would be in it, "for a bit of the crack to while the time away." She liked to talk at the end of a day.

In they'd come and sit down, often in silence. Then, "Sharp weather," they might say out of the blue. "There's little change now from the days." ". . . Aye, it's not a hard life if you don't weaken." Things like that.

Bachelor men, some with bone-white hair, wandered down from the hills, old men of the road on their way to the convent, a tinker or gypsy seeking directions, maybe a neighbouring farmer needing a hand with a cow who was calving or with a horse which had run away.

As the farmhouse lay by the crossroads, it seemed to serve as a halfway station for the whole townland. There'd be chance comers and goers late into the evening. And never a car, rare enough then, went by than Cissie wasn't up to the window, remarking its history, a fuller account following as she sat back down by the fire.

"Glory be to goodness, that was your big man the Yank, bless the creature, back from the town. Wonder of wonders, that's the second trip in today. Sure, isn't it himself is having the time of his life? They say he may settle, though, for her in her high heels. Dickens the bit of it, I'm thinking. It's a fine soft life she has . . ." And the talk then moved that way, every one of them chipping away at the outline of the figure the returned Yank cut among them, not at home with the matter of him, he'd been so much away.

Or it could be the vet. You knew if it were the priest or the doctor out on a sick call, before she uttered a word, for she crossed herself in returning. Some old farmer was not long for the world. "The priest's annointed him, I had wind of it only this morning from the creamery man." So now they reckoned up the old man's earthly possessions, distributing them out as to how they thought they'd best fall. "Aye, be big money, do you know like, for a long man he was. Pete should have some, but he's dead and gone now, a decenter man there never was. How like the father he was – a quiet class of a man, kept to himself like, lived with the mother. Not the brother, though, had a bit of the devil in him. Oh aye, I mind him well. You'd have come across him, he's dead and gone now too, this many's a day. What year would that be?"

Then they sat often lapsed into silence, respecting the fire till one or other was inclined again to speak, not necessarily in sequence but as though moved by the spirit. They threw down their words in the very same manner you saw them slap down their money, closing a deal on the town's market day. Minding tales of old, of inheritances lost, hens and cows spirited away, of harvests gone by, of what was happening down Belfast way. They spoke as actors, deliberately, timing their moves, sometimes pausing to spit some long-chewed tobacco straight into the heart of the flames. It made quite a hiss when it landed.

We young ones sat quietly, taking in every detail, I suppose, half-aware even then, of a way of life that was gone.

"God reward you, Daughter, aren't you the wee bonnie lass," they'd say when we handed them a cup of tea. The old country folk called everyone "Daughter" regardless of gender or age. Quiet men, they were not at ease with questions and answers, they simply offered up their own musings while intent on the flames.

Sometimes Your Da himself might turn up if he had a run in his cab out that way. He'd give us a look questioning why we were still up, but he never interfered, knowing it was our home from home the whole summer through. Cissie rarely harped on on the matter of bedtimes. "Sure, makes not a ha'porth of odds, you'd be up with the lark anyway."

"True enough," says Your Da, puffing on his pipe.

And up you were too, for you had your own cow to milk. It was one of the first things you did on arrival, choosing your cow for your stay.

All the cows had names in those days. There was always a Bluebell, a Buttercup, a Polly, and Daisy, a Black Molly, a Strawberry and Roan, a Snowball and the Kerry Blue, others being cousins removed, if it were a big herd. You were up at the crack of dawn for their milking.

Cissie's way of alarm in the morning was to sing up the stairs, "John – John, the Grey Goose has gone," and, you rose, sleepy-eyed, to get to your cow and your three-legged stool in the stalls, tripping unsteadily after Matt down the stairs. We were not very good at the milking, more muddling along.

One morning Bluebell, my cow of the time, was in a mood of her own, maybe caused by the bow I'd tied on her tail. It became a disaster.

"Ahem! God of God. Would yez take its foot from

the bucket," cried Matt. Bluebell did it herself with a sizable kick, landing the whole pail of frothy milk the far side of the byre.

Joe, Micky and Pat as one were collapsed in convulsions, their own buckets in jeopardy.

"It's got a tick in its teat, you dope, you big townie dope. It's what comes from moving it around like a filly lamb," screamed Micky in between his guffaws. That was true enough too. We girls often removed our cows from the common herd, and took them from field to field throughout the day, to give them, as we saw it, more grass and more care. They'd be on the hoof half the day. The fields themselves had names then. You could move Bluebell or Daisy from the Mountainy field, to the Sally Willow by the river, over into the Rowan field or back up the hill to the one with the yellow whins.

If Matt were off to a buying fair early, Micky was appointed to take charge of the milking. On arrival in the byre we'd find a bullock apiece, tied up in the place of our cows, a chance for him to prove – as he so often reckoned – that we soft townie girls couldn't tell the difference between the two beasts.

Milking time then fell away into abandon, with Micky revelling in his appointment from beginning to end, and the creamery van had to wait, making every farm in the parish late for the day.

"God help us, you're a card, a star turn," was all Cissie said to him on her return, shaking her head.

We girls, I suppose, had an easy deal out there at Cissie's, helping round the house, churning the milk, printing the butter, collecting and washing the eggs, picking the rhubarb and goosegabs, helping with the hay-making teas, chasing butterflies, blowing suds with dandelion stalks . . . it never seemed like work at all, and Cissie never came back empty-handed from market day in the town. There could be a jigsaw or a humming top in all shades of colours, a new sheet of transfers, or a big bag of sherbet with a dollop of toffee on a stick to do for a dipper.

And one day a week came the seedsman's travelling shop. A van as big as a house, it sold all that was wanted. When Cissie and Matt had cleared the business of feed stuffs and bone meal for the pigs, the cows, and the hens, and had had the news of the whole townlands, we were bidden in to choose something for ourselves.

It was hard, for one side of the van was fitted out like a chemist's shop, in wee neat wooden drawers with only the van man knowing for sure what each had inside. Like a lucky dip, they were filled up with buttons or bows, ointments, worming powders or lint. We had to give up in the end, and ask for any broken biscuits, comics, or boiled sweets.

As the van man carried no small weighing scales, we did very well. After closing transactions for a fortune's worth of meals, "It'd be a tight man indeed," said Cissie, "seen to measure out a few ha'porth of sweets."

Often you ended with no choice at all, getting a mixed bag of aniseed balls, cinnamon, pear or acid drops, the comics, and a novelty or trinket, produced in a trice from the far side of the van, a gay plastic windmill, a grey clockwork mouse, or a packet of coloured plasticine, the same as the churned butter patted all into pleats.

One of the farm's fields had a grove of wych-elm trees in a ring in the middle. This, already well hidden in hawthorn, we took for a camp. It was quite a way from the house and the bull was often in there, lending added acclaim. With some neighbouring children we made a very fine camp, in time spreading from leafy branch to branch. One afternoon "Yup Yup" Matt arrived out of the blue to fetch the bull, and saw us aloft. He stood like a post.

"Jesus, Mary and Joseph, will yez come down from the tree? Bless us and save us, what are ye at?

You'll set the "Wee Folk" on top of us,

For the milk to go sour,

The cows to go lame,

The horse run away.

Ahem! Do you hear me, will yez come out of the trees?"

It was a long speech for Matt, a regular litany, as if learnt of old from his own mother's knee. With slanty looks at each other we slid down one by one, pondering the while that there was maybe more to these culchie folk, as we townies called country people, than at first did appear. And all over the head of a couple of trees.

Pestering Cissie later, she gave us no pity, but left us in deeper mystery still.

"It's no good your coming to me. Divil the bit of it. For it is the lore of the land, as old as the hills. From time immemorial everyone in the whole townlands knows you don't meddle, go footering in Fairy Rings, the older Gods' graves." There she ended.

Joe's solution was to go on a dig, Micky acting watch, while we others looked on. But the most that he found buried there was bits of old farm machinery and the broken-down horns of what he thought was a ram.

When Matt and Cissie were about, the Fairy Thorn camp, for no good earthly cause, stayed well and truly out of play.

All in all, it was a much fought-over holiday out there at Cissie's and Matt's. We usually went, two or three at a time, for a fortnight or so. Cissie believed in elbow grease. If you were a good worker, you might be asked to stay on. Joe, fit as a fiddle, often stayed a whole month. "A visitor to your own home," Your Ma said of him as he cycled in to see her on the town's market day. I think she was a little jealous, looking back, for she took a certain pride in her eldest son. But Cissie and she were really friends of the first order. They couldn't make enough of each other. Cissie was forever planning wee treats for Your Ma.

One bright summer's day, she decided to take our mother for a spin up to the border. They'd have a good day's shopping and tea in an hotel. To go across the Northern border, to the Republic, was a great outing then, and Matt set out to drive them. He drove after a fashion, but never did concede the gears of a car. These constantly needed replacing from his crashing. "Bad cess to them," he'd say. "Sure, ahem! I can't get the hang of the creatures at all."

Joe and Miss Eilish, who were staying out there at the time, saw the opportunity to send home secretly a mother duck with her new yellow ducklings. They hid them in the boot of Matt's car. But the plan went haywire, and those ducklings also went for a spin up to the border.

While Matt was crashing the gears, the ducklings couldn't be heard. Then they stopped at the customs' post.

"Anything to declare?" asked the customs man.

"No, officer," replied Cissie. Anyone in a uniform was an officer to Cissie.

It was then that the quacking started, "Quack, quack," went those ducklings in chorus.

"And what have you in your boot then, missus?" he inquired.

"Glory be to God and the Holy Angels, I don't know and that's the truth of it," said she, or so our mother recounted later.

"You don't think that broody hen, you mind the one that ran away, would have nested there?" she whispers to my mother.

"Well, I think we had better open up and make sure," says he. When he saw the duck and her ducklings, he cautioned her: "The smuggling of fowl over the Northern border into the Irish Republic is an offence of the very first order."

"Them children!" says Cissie, "the big bold articles, they have my heart scalded, wait till I get my hands on them." But the upshot was that the customs man obliged, and kept the mother and her ducklings in a box in his customs post until they passed back that way in the evening.

Months were to pass before Joe and Miss Eilish were restored to a full state of grace out there.

"Don't mention ducklings to me," Joe told us, attempting not to smile. Joe often rode up on Cissie's big rough farm horse, tying it outside our front door while he visited. He didn't waste time if Your Ma or Da were not to be found, hooves clip-clopping on up the street.

"Tell them I came and no one answered. Adios amigos, Howdy Townie Pardners," and as cool as sixpence he was gone. Once I think he brought Your Ma a bunch of flowers.

"From me," he said awkwardly, and rode away again.

4

In the holidays we were forever trying to smuggle home farm animals to the town. Red Ned was acquired that way. He had been a very fine rooster out in the country, but he took a turn for the worse and got out of hand in the town. We gave him a hutch in our back yard, but he soon ruled the roost, flying and pecking at anyone who went out there. My mother couldn't get her washing out or in. Even Your Da's building programme was held up.

"That rooster will be the death's scourge of me," Your Ma did cry. "Is there no one will rid me of it?" she'd sigh. Miss Sean, very loyally, and with certain bravery, caught it, and pulled its neck, and for his trouble became known ever more as Pierpoint the Executioner.

With Red Ned gone, Your Ma could get back to her washing line and her garden. This she was very proud of, and with every cause. There were not many gardens in back yards those days, and Your Ma's was a thing of beauty, smelling sweet, with its nasturtiums, wallflowers and sweet allysum, her favourites. There had been a bit of a barney when she had taken over some ground of our play yard in its making.

As our street stood at the rise of a hill, there was a big sheer drop of fifty feet or so from our back yard to a large, derelict area below. In fact, down there was also owned by Your Da. He'd had to buy it in the house deal, but it was ruled over by some old targer, who wouldn't let him or anyone else in through her entry for its use. When she loosed her tongue even Your Da fled.

"She'd stare the sun in the face, that one," sighed my mother.

"Say nothing," says Your Da. "I don't like to hear a woman that way," was all Your Da ever said, waiting for her to wear out her tongue. She never did.

We children, gazing down from the dizzy heights of our back wall, used to eye the land below enviously and, through the lack of it, often our games spilled over into Your Ma's garden. The boys tunnelled there, looking for snails for the snail-game or worms for fishing. They tunnelled too well, for one day Your Ma's garden, the whole lot of it, about thirty feet long, disappeared, falling away into the derelict land below. Your Ma just stood surveying the wreckage. "I don't know. Atrocious! This is too much altogether." Your Da had to be sent for. Miss Kilian was dispatched to the carstands for him.

"You're to come quick, Your Ma's garden's disappeared," he was told. The other taxi-men shook their heads in wonderment, it seemed, but they were used to it, as he was always being sent for. A new wall had to be built. My mother told the story well. "It's a mercy of God I'm here to tell the tale, I might have gone with it," the obvious run-on line being, if half the tunnellers had done just that, they'd have only been getting their just deserts.

Many many times I went to fetch Your Da.

"You're to come home quick. Miss Kilian's done something bad." He moved the pipe slowly sideways.

"How bad is bad?"

"Too bad to say."

"I see, I'll be home presently then."

The seaside lay only six miles away, so, on a summer's day with a patch of blue at all, we were off to the sea for a dip. When younger we went by train. We taller ones crowded close to the ticket office asking for, "Four halfs please", while pushing through the small ones, made wee by stooping, like we played in the "Stalky Bluebell" game. This procedure we repeated at the open-air baths where everyone swam. The turnstile here was a bit more complicated, and some eejit or other often got stuck in it. So we'd be caught, let off with a warning, but have no money for a poke of ice-cream.

Miss Malachy was rarely with us at this stage. You'd have found him still standing on the home station, waiting for a particular train. Being a train lover, he only went on certain ones.

"The 'Big Dinky' one's coming through today from

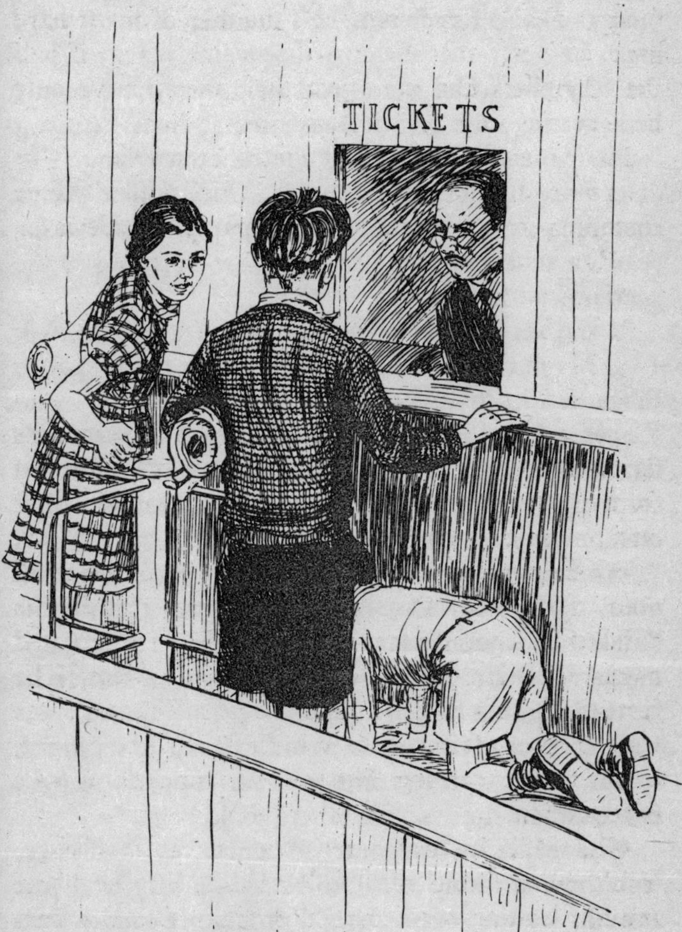
TICKETS

the South, I just know it," he'd sigh. So there we would leave him with his shy smile, standing all by himself on the now deserted platform, waiting for the "Big Dinky" or for "No. 11", another of his joys in life.

Every one of us were good swimmers, and as the baths were built on the seashore, at high tide you could use the spring board the other way round to dive straight into the open sea. Our mother was a champion swimmer, she did the competition swim for years, a mile out and back it was. We could never keep up.

At the very height of summer when Your Da took Your Ma out for the odd evening run in the car, Miss Eilish, left in charge, dashed in straight away to make supper as they both drove off. All down the years we felt as hard done by on supper as we did with those chips. We never really had one officially like other children in the street did.

"You're wanted in for your supper," the street cries used to go. Your Da always said it was really their dinner but no doubt with bought chips it didn't merit the name. But especially when younger, we suffered a lot through that lack of supper.

In no time, Miss Eilish would call out to us in the street, "You're all to come in, your supper's ready," at least a few times so the others could hear.

"Supper," we'd repeat to ourselves endlessly, savouring the word, "I'll be back in a jiffy, I'm just away in for me supper," we'd pronounce loudly with great pride.

Inside Miss Eilish would have laid out great plates

of thick buttered bread with syrup and a dusting of sugar on top, which was what we all thought supper was about and a big jug of milky cocoa to wash the lot down. To us, sheer bliss!

And she'd have tried to make chips in Your Ma's biggest frying pan, but they were often burnt to a cinder and not up to much. And as our mother as bad as our Da disowned vinegar, they lacked the right taste. She wouldn't give house room to vinegar, "for it brings you no good and thins down the blood into the bargain," so she said of it.

Back on the street, we'd pretend we'd had bought chips, vinegar, the lot.

"Falone's chips are going down the hill a wee bit, don't you think? Changed the vinegar, I expect," we'd say to the others outside. There were two chip shops in the town, both run by Italians.

Towards the end of summer, Your Da took us on a day's traditional outing to the seaside, not the one with the swimming baths, but way round the coast, and noted for the shells and the sand. Your Ma was up making sandwiches from the crack of dawn. Ten loaves or so she'd use in their making. Then, along with big car and tractor tubes all blown up for the sea, we'd pile into one or two black cabs and be on our way.

There were so many of us in there, we girls often got sick. "The Three Dying Swans", Your Da called us as he stopped, yet again, to let one of us out.

"I think they're crocking again," beseeched Your Ma. Your Da's big smoky pipe didn't help us a bit.

On the beach, we built wee sandcastles and always,

always, someone got stung by a jellyfish. It happened each time. Our Granny could cure it. "Granny-Granny-Grey-Beard" often came along with us, just for the spin. It was the one day a year she let her hair down. Dapple-grey and unbraided, it fell to her waist.

Your Da never swam, he just paddled his feet, but the rest of us floated round on the big tractor tyre, with Your Ma in the middle.

Often by home time, with the tide gone away, we'd grow very bored.

"But what can we do now?" we'd beg of Your Ma.

"Oh, go and find gold now!" she cried once in desperation. We did just that and found her a fine golden chain, which she wore for always round her neck. So now we were serious about it, "Searching for Gold" on the out-going tide. But we never struck lucky again.

And then, summer gone, the holidays came to an end, and it was back to school again.

5

Granny-Granny-Grey-Beard was our mother's mother. She lived in the country. A couple of us often cycled out there after school to pay her a visit or take her a message.

She had got as a young girl, we were told, a bit of a needle stuck in her thigh, somehow; so she always hobbled on a cane. "Oh, it's the needle," she'd cry, with a sharp gasp of pain, as we children followed her round the farmyard, where she showed us the new calves or the chicks.

"She's rusting. Not worth her salt that one," she'd say, pointing her stout stick at some unfortunate hen or other who wasn't doing her stuff. All of us children nodded thoughtfully, not having a notion of what she was talking.

Just after the war, Joe and Miss Eilish had been sent out as we'ans, to stay with her for a while. They had meddled their way into her good front room and were found playing sandcastles with all her precious bags of sugar and tea that had been sent to her from America. She never got over it, it vexed her so. To her dying day she was still "minding" them of the way they'd "blotted their copybooks" on their first ever visit.

She was a great one for the cures, our granny. People came from miles round for the cure of the sprain she had. At such times we children, if visiting, were shooed outside, but we often managed to hang around unseen. There was a lot of mixing of meal (mail as she called it) and buttermilk and a mumbling of words which we took to be prayers. And the callers never came or left empty-handed.

"How are you doing in your books? Can you say all your lessons? Are you a good scholar? They don't put the dunce's cap on ye, I hope?" she'd ask. Culchie talk of the very first magnitude. It was how the old country folk spoke. We took note of it for future use in the town.

"Riddle me this out now. Divil the use, them seeing glasses of mine," she'd say, holding up some thin airmail letter from her son far away in America.

She was a great one, too, for the ghost stories. There was, I remember, one about the Headless Coachman and Four. One of her kinsmen, centuries back, had crossed paths with it while making his way homeward from market in his horse and cart: "And on certain nights of the year when the moon is away, as sure as I'm standing here, you can hear those chains."

Everyone seemed to have grannies those days.

They'd be dressed all in black and usually knitting. They taught you that too, on your first wooden needles.

> *"In thro' the bunny hole
> Round the big tree
> Out thro' the bunny hole
> And off pops she."*

They'd sing as they did it.

Granny-Granny-Grey-Beard was a prize crocheter and knitter. At school you were taught it too. Next after learning to be good and kind, the nuns took the knitting lesson very, very, seriously. It was always socks that you knitted. Mine were for Your Da and bright turquoise in colour. Granny-Granny-Greybeard helped pick up my dropped stitches but went away on, on her own, well past the heel. Only she turned it the square way that wasn't allowed. The nuns did it different, usually round.

I was in such fear and dread to show it at school that I just went on knitting. It got to such a size that it needed a shoe box all to its own. I couldn't go up to learn how to cast off for the toe, so square was that heel.

Your Ma put her foot down, finally, about the money for wool. "You can't need another ball, two-ply, three-ply, plain or purl," she cried. "Honest to God, you'd swear you were knitting a house." Little did she know the drapery shop itself had run out. In the way of these things, all was discovered and ripped out, in wee curly blue woollen lines.

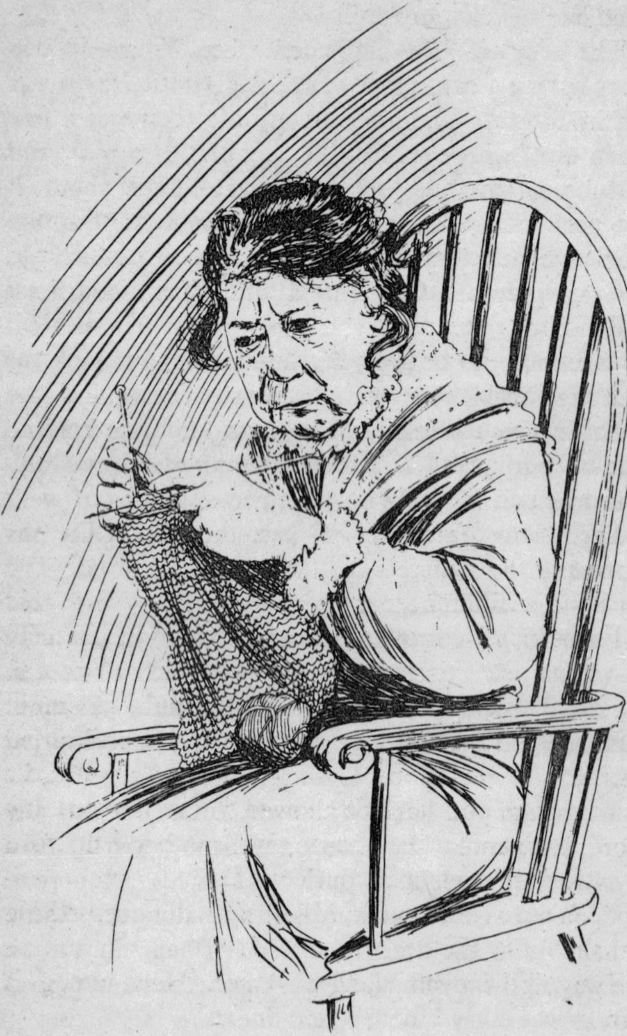

Granny-Granny-Grey-Beard was a terror for always going on about things you didn't want known, like what had befallen my doll.

The accident had happened when Your Ma was away having a baby. Her sister, our Auntie Mary, was left in control. The pride of my life then was a fine china doll, with eyes of blue, lips red as a rose, and with head, arms and legs that could all move about. It got such play that one day the elastic contraption inside which held all on, snapped, and the doll's limbs and head flew asunder. Our Auntie Mary stood stock still in horror like me.

"Saints preserve us, Your Da mustn't know," was her first and last response. Together we hid the remains in an old leather trunk upstairs. This episode was then referred to for evermore, as the Trunk Murder.

For a long time after, I fled when Your Da was around.

"It's generations since I've seen you play with that nice wee doll I got you," he'd say slyly, so eventually all was owned up to and the doll sent away by post to the dolls' hospital in the city. In the course of time it returned home like a new pin and was soon knitted out for the season by Granny-Granny-Grey-Beard's skill, though you weren't allowed to call her that any more. I remember the occasion well, as it was my turn to cycle to the carstands for Your Da.

"You're to come quick, Miss Sean's done something wrong."

The pipe moved slowly; "I see. How wrong is wrong?"

"He called Granny-Granny-Grey-Beard, Granny-Granny-Grey-Beard to Your Ma's face."

There was half a smile, "I see."

I turned to go.

"By the way," he inquired, "What do you call her as a rule?"

I looked at him, puzzled. "Why, Granny-Granny-Grey-Beard, of course, like you."

"I see. Sounds like it's time we put a stop to that," and shaking with great laughter, he told me to skip off.

6

And then with a drop in the length of the days it was autumn, the fruit full and the blackberry season suddenly upon us. The word spread. Usually someone rode into our street on a bike and skidded to a halt. "Blackberries have arrived, and you'd better believe it!" From every house then in the street, children could be seen looking out buckets and pails, tin cans and jam jars, any container at all, for collecting the berries. For there was money to be made, one of the few times a year. "And we're not talking pennies here, there's a mint to be had," as the big bike boys said.

Gangs and rival gangs formed, bigger boys in charge, wee'er ones included, with strict instructions, if they didn't do what they were told to do, they might as well leave now. And off we set. Weekends were best, there being no school, Sundays included when you'd changed from your good going-to-Mass clothes.

We'd take thick doorsteps of sandwiches made by

ourselves, all parcelled up in greaseproof paper, to do us for lunch. You rarely brought drinks. There was always a trickling stream about, and if your sandwiches ran out or met with an accident, you could eat berries from the woods with the bread and cheese leaves of the sweet-smelling hawthorn tree.

Outside our small town, in any direction, the country began. The favourite way out was up past the big boys' school towards Windy Hill, taking in an area vaguely described as the Quarries – a scene of many adventures, and tragedy as well, for children had drowned there. You'd be warned to steer clear of the Blue Motion itself, one particular water-logged quarry with a terrible history. It was a place to avoid, known of old to generations of boys and their fathers before them. We obeyed without question. You did, I suppose, in those days.

Straightening up, Joe would pronounce, "Right-o then, let's go. About turn," and march his group forward in a military manner, all of them hanging on to the side of a rope so as to keep in line. They'd salute as they struck off down the street.

It was a real laugh but in many ways Joe kept the lot of us on our toes. And with good cause, for later on that day maybe we'd be chased by a witch.

The witch lived in a field in a bluebell wood, in a great barn of a house as seen from the distance. Years past, two steady boys from the town, not fancy-prone, nor notion-led, out blackberrying, had been chased by herself and her hounds. They appeared back later in their own street in a terrible state, all black and blue, scratched head to foot and empty-handed, their buckets abandoned in their flight. Two fine milking-pails they'd been and these recovered later, miles from the spot, were found then to be kicked in and battered beyond any known repair. They recounted the tale for years. "Ah you should have seen her . . ." We believed it all.

Few ventured into the witch's field. It was a lone place. We all of us hugged close to ditches for a fast getaway, if one should be neeeded. Not knowing which way she'd be coming but certain she was.

Safe past the witch's field, there'd be a mad race to find the best bushes. Gangs could be seen hurtling over stone ditches at breakneck speed. Little ones tore their legs on the brambles as they stumbled in vain to keep up. They'd rush to the bushes, often only to find others had beaten them to it. Tall children ambled, taking their time and the pick of the high blackberries only they could reach.

Towards late afternoon, all met up by Windy Hill. Sitting in the shadow of a big duckie stone known as "Rocky Mountain", we'd show off our blackberries. Buckets were passed from hand to hand in an attempt to value their worth.

What cries of admiration greeted the sight of the juicy black ones, overflowing from the bigger boys' buckets. What scorn was cast on littler children's jam jars, and little girls' seaside pails. These were often barely full and contained a mixture of reddish and ("Holy God" cried the experts "even green berries at that,") many still with the stems fully attached. "That's a blackberry. Ye tell me that." – "Y'er jokin'."

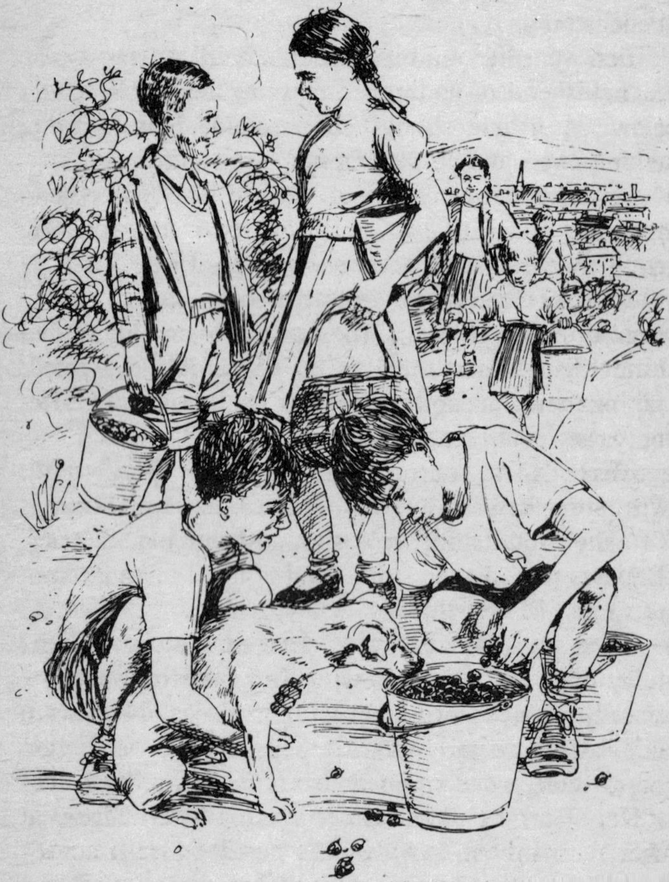

Often, though, older children would take pity, and carefully dole out a few of their own big bruisers ("That's one and no mistake") in the hope of veiling the little bucket's nakedness, and their own embarrassment to be, "Mother of God," as they put it, "seen in such company, going back into town."

Then we'd sit for a bit on the high hill, there where the fields ended, looking down on the small town below. Munching the last of any sandwiches before making our way homewards and to the spirit-grocers who bought berries. There we watched as he weighed them, never questioning at all, happy to be paid two bright thrupenny-bits for a big bucketful.

Every penny-bit was money those days. Those seasonal earnings were not to be scorned. Many children got no pocket money at all.

In our own family's case, Your Da brought home a big bag of sweets, one evening a week, which he transferred to a tall frosted glass jar. The town's best sweet shop was by the carstands, so he never forgot. We called it Sweet Evening as he passed round the Dippeys, named more for the use of your hands, not your eyes, in their choice. It was a blind dip. You'd be vexed, if at your turn you came up with a handful of jujubes. This softer variety was only fit, we considered, for we'ans in nappies or grannies old as old, both at the jelly-baby stage of life.

But those sweets were never enough. We were forever searching new ways of making Sweet Money. After school there was always a headlong dash home to get the skins-bucket first. This was a pail of leftovers which could be sold to the shop that kept pigs down the back. Whoever was lucky made off with it up the street for all they were worth, spilling most as they ran. Others in full pursuit tried to pull the pail from their hands, spilling half the rest. There'd be a whole trail of potato peelings and such in a wavy wee line following right behind.

7

And the year went on. Soon autumn was gone, and Christmas was upon us. It was a grand time in our family. Your Ma was a very fine cook and a great upholder of festive traditions. She had cakes for every occasion, and the power of both hands in their beating. When she was young, she scalded one hand feeding new calves, so she'd had to learn how to work with both equally. We'd have a shamrock-green iced cake for St Patrick's day, one with daffodil-yellow icing to celebrate Easter, but best of all we loved her Christmas cakes.

They were always the same, and she made quite a few. Her fanciest-iced one was where she made oval lace shapes, piping the icing first on to the back of a spoon. As lightly as possible, she transferred them to the cake. We all held our breath in case they broke. Another had a small mirror for a lake embedded in the rough snow icing, on which she then placed some dashing American skaters. But the cake I liked best was one she never white-iced at all; she just coloured more marzipan, red and green, for the holly berries and leaves, and tied round a bright red ribbon for the finishing touch.

Her Christmas puddings she did as of old, hiding silver thrupenny bits and buttons in the mixture. We each had a token stir before the puddings were tied up in white linen cloths. They'd be bubbling for hours on the range. Finally a big round ball of a pudding appeared on a plate, with a skin thick as leather, growing dark and glossy while we watched. You could see the shapes of the cherries, sultanas, raisins, and currants settling beneath. She'd put a big holly sprig on the top.

Your Da, on one of his regular runs to the country, had weeks ago eyemarked his turkey.

"Oh boys, oh boys, she's coming on nicely out there. Would set your heart singing," he'd tell us. He took a great pride in the size of his bird. They got bigger and bigger down the years until they could hardly fit in the oven at all. Your Ma finally put her foot down, threatening to send them away to the baker's, like the skinny-link people who ate chips.

Christmas Eve was one of the officially silent evenings in our house, more or less. After helping put up the decorations, nail up the holly, bring out the crib, watch Your Ma check on her puddings, pin frills round the cakes, the lot of us were subjected to a fierce scrubbing till faces shone, and were banished to bed early with our stockings, under pain of Santa Claus knowing if we did misbehave.

From our rooms we sang out in chorus our own renderings of carols.

> *"Once in Royal Joey's City*
> *Stood a lowly cattle shed*
> *Where your Mother laid out Babynun*
> *Beside, Big Head, in his bed . . ."*

Or we might sing them in Latin, we knew quite a few.

Nobody, true believer or not, ventured downstairs. Only Miss Bronagh had managed that once. It was her moment now; she made quite a few deals on Christmas Eve night, in the telling.

There'd be first a quiet tap on the floor, then, "Miss Bronagh, can you hear me down there? I'll give you quite a few chocolates from my big box from Santa tomorrow if you tell us again," we'd beg.

"Now, what did he look like? Did Your Ma give him tea?" And Miss Bronagh proudly recited up the whole tale all over again, floor to floor.

Our favourite presents were Snow Houses. They came in all shapes: a clock with a face, a gypsy caravan or Santa himself all covered in white cottonwool. The trick was to find the wee secret door and get out the small presents hidden within, wrapped up in bright tissue paper.

We tried to keep awake for as long as we could, but in the end fell asleep, though with nine of us that never lasted long. Slowly but steadily the familiar sounds began, the click of a light switch, the creak of a door, soft voices at first, "Hey, what did he bring you?" echoing from wall to wall. Often there were big toys like bikes, or army jeeps. The boys started riding them all round the rooms. There were big boxes of chocolates of many different sorts. One Christmas, I recall, the King got ones made of ginger.

"Holy Jeepers," he cried out quite vexed. "I'm sure he's made a mistake. They must have been meant for Your Ma's cookery cupboard downstairs." But no matter what they were made of, we never ate a one, not even a lick. You were fasting those days for Communion in the morning.

In no time every light was on, and it was one hullabaloo, with doors banging all over the place.

"If you don't quit that racket and get back into bed, this minute, this moment, this instant – now!" cried Your Ma up the stairs, "I'll tell him to come back and take the whole lot away. I'm sure he's not left the street yet, I can still catch him, give him the nod."

"Holy smoke, what's going on up there? A bit of order now!" shouts Your Da.

For a while all was silent. From each room in turn could just be heard the crackling of stiff glassy paper, torn away in the dark.

I think of one Christmas Eve long ago, when I invited Miss Bronagh to sleep in my room, instead of her normal abode below with Miss Eilish. In the dead of night, slowly, I swapped her presents over while she continued to sleep.

"Did you like the wee toy gas cooker he left you?" asked Your Ma in the morning.

"Oh, he gave Miss Bronagh that," I tried, "I've got wee twin dolls with their mother attached."

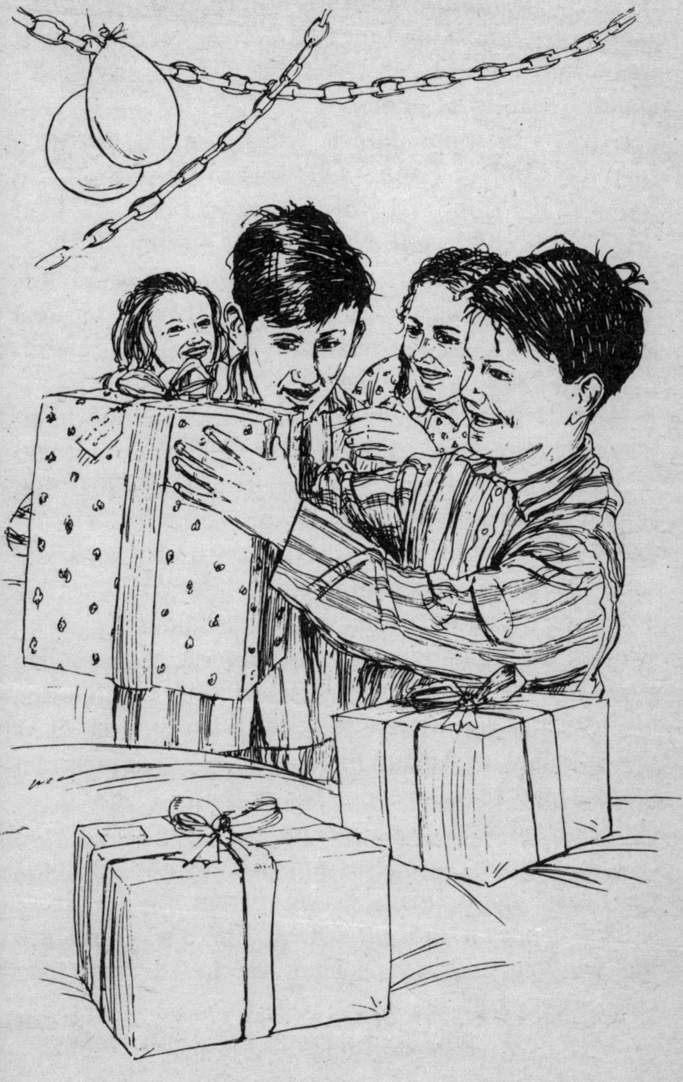

"Have you indeed?" Despite the danger of letting on all that she knew, Your Ma still righted the wrong.

At official morning time, we were all off to Mass. It was a long one too, on Christmas Day morning. We couldn't wait to be home.

Before Christmas dinner, which we ate late, we'd play the Orphan Game. This was my invention. I'd found in the front of a Howard Spring book, the line: "And those children fled away in the storm . . ."

It caught the heart just the right way, and was quickly adopted as a Family Refrain. If there was real trouble about, we all sadly sighed, "And those children fled away in the storm."

It came into its own late on Christmas morning, when the street, often snow white and deserted, was as a stage only lit from the wings. Your Da's Christmas timing suited us well – the darker the better. The lot of us slipped away into the street, and eyemarked some bright festive dwelling.

Taking up station there, we huddled outside, gazing steadily through its good front window to the warm glow beyond, cursing the crib or tree which often blocked the view. There we stood silently, each of us trying to look as sad and forlorn and ill-fed as possible, murmuring to ourselves, the refrain, "And those children fled away in the storm . . ."

"Oh, the poor wee dotes and on a day like this too," we heard some unsuspecting parent say, and we smiled as one. A first hit scored! There was a rush to the window and door. Then we heard their own children cry back.

"Oh no, it's only that pack of daft eejits from way

up the street." By which time we were gone, on our way to another, in giggles, but shadows fading into the gloom, following the dim form of Joe dragging his feet.

Joe and Miss Eilish were the best at The Orphan Game. Joe could easily look aloof, pale and consumptive, and he had perfected a limp, leaning on one of us like he'd forgotten his crutches. Miss Eilish, in a plaid shawl, would cradle Babynun or Miss Connor, adept as any gypsy on the town's market day, with her eyes downcast and two big tears at the corner of them.

Mission complete, we'd slip in back home unseen. One occasion stands out, when Your Da suddenly drove up alongside us.

"Holy Moses, see what I see?" said Miss Kilian.

"Don't run or we're all ruined," Joe took over.

"And what has you out with not a sinner about?" inquired Your Da, winding the car window down.

"Checking the chimney for the fire."

"It's not gone out?" asks Your Da, in alarm about his pride and joy.

Joe shook his head. He'd read Your Da right. In a cloud of pipe smoke, he was already driving on to make sure.

Christmas dinner was enormous, and you couldn't rust at it. Your Da liked good eaters.

"That's my fellow," he'd say of any boy, man enough for third helpings of turkey and ham and sirloin of beef. "Sure, they don't eat like they used to," he'd sigh sadly. "Now when I was your age, let me just tell you, this wouldn't have been the half of it. It would have been only what you might call the introduction." He put a great emphasis on the word as he said it. "Aye, we ate like Trojans, slept like heroes then."

Later, chock-full, we collapsed into the good front room, where we played the Game, as we called Bagatelle, or put on wee plays.

We girls would be asked to recite. The three of us went to elocution classes, once a week after school, where you learned how to do this.

"You sound more like a culchie than ever before," was Joe's verdict on us. There were two elocution teachers in the town. Miss Eilish, for some reason, went to the grand one, Miss Bronagh and I made do with the other.

When the town Feis was on, there was great rivalry between those teachers as to who won most medals and mentions. They choose different poems. That Christmas Miss Eilish's piece was *My Papa has a Jaguar*.

My Papa has a Jaguar
And Pa drives rather fast
Flying castles do abound as we go driving past . . .

She got no further.

"Your Papa has a big ugly brute of a taxi-cab which always needs cleaning," threw in Joe as she tripped the lines daintily on her tongue.

Miss Bronagh and I together did *The Witch*.

I saw her plucking cowslips
And marked her where she stood

She never knew I watched her while hiding in the wood.
Her face was bright as crimson and black her steeple hat
Her broomstick lay beside her, I'm positive of that . . .

"A couple of right eejits the pair of you, if you can't tell a spade from a broomstick. Sure, it was only an ole Culchie-woman working her potato patch late of an evening," was Joe's verdict on us, the original big brother with that faint smile of superiority like he couldn't really help it, he was just born that way. But we girls sighed for him, "It was but he was jealous."

For the town's Feis was such a big day. You wore your First Communion frock, your hair taken care of, done up in white ribbons. You missed school, too. Boys rarely entered. Lord Mucks or Little Boy Blues they were called if they did, which left Joe and the others out of it.

The adjudicator sat on a big wooden throne, so many fates in his hands while you waited your turn for the stage. We won a few medals over the years, silver and bronze, never gold. We knew in our hearts that the boys were the medal winners.. They won them for sports, often beating each other to do it. The evidence was hanging right there before us, all round the walls of that good Christmas room.

As we knew too, it would be Joe's turn before long to perform. At some stage of the Christmas proceedings, Your Da always called for him to sing him his own favourite song. Joe had a clear sweet voice, and he sang the song movingly over the years. I can still see Your Ma with a gentle smile on her lips, Your Da with a fierce pride in his eyes, at the end suddenly getting up to poke the fire. But not now.

"Right, Joe, we'll have the *Castle of Dromore*."

In a mood of his own these days, Joe chose silence, looking for a way out. A look passed between mother and son, then, rubbing his big nose, he tried.

*"October winds lament around the Castle of Dromore
Yet peace is in her lofty halls, aphais de' ban a stor.
Though autumn leaves may droop and die
A bard of spring are you
Singing hushabye lul, lul-lo, lo-lah, singing husha
. . ."*

He stopped, sang nothing. It was no use.

"Kilian, take over," said Your Da. It was the first time that had ever happened. Eagerly Kilian began.

*"October winds lament around the Castle of Dromore.
Yet peace is in her lofty halls, aphais de' ban a . . ."*

Someone smiled, someone laughed. Hit by a fit of coughing, Kilian came to a stop.

"Sean," says Your Da.

"October winds lament around the Castle of Dromore yet peace . . ."

Spluttering, Sean stopped. Everyone was by now giggling their heads off, yet on it went.

Malachy got as far as *"October winds lament . . ."* when Your Da declared a full halt to the proceedings.

"Lament is right! Has it come to this? What have I bred at all? Ye think a man having reared an army of them, not every man can say as much – and not a singer among them . . ."

"Well, I don't know, this here family," sighed Your Ma sadly.

And though she rounded off Christmas night as always, telling stories of days long long ago, into the evening, you knew that Christmas night had been different somehow.

8

Every day of our lives followed a pattern, the church and its seasons colouring all. There seemed to be bells tolling the whole day long, Angelus Bells, Joy Bells, ones for Evening Devotions, Benediction, Confraternities, Holy Hours, visiting the "Monstrance", St Patrick's day parades, Corpus Christi processions, Penal Mass rocks, always something of a devotional nature to attend.

You had it in school as well. The nuns were a terror. What with May Altars, wee holy cribs, feast days and name days, you never seemed to have a minute to get on with your homework. You'd no sooner knitted or gathered something together for their Christmas than a name day or feast day made its way round. The name days were special, and they chose very odd ones. We had Mothers Ignatius and Innocent, Mother Mary Baptist, Immaculata, Assumpta, Fidelis, on and on they went. You couldn't imagine there being nuns without those names.

The country girls could always bring in big armfuls of flowers. Bluebells and violets carpeted the woods, and there were thick masses of primroses, whin blossom even, just for the taking out there. But in the town we had to save our penny-pieces for flowers. On the whole, though, we girls were sad as sad when we left the nuns to go to the big schools, where there were few of them around. Then there were ordinary teachers with tough reputations. You'd long for the name days, the knitting and altars, though at least now your prayers were your own. The nuns were always begging them off you, for their patron saints, for someone in limbo or to add in last minute to a spiritual bouquet for the Holy Father, the Pope.

The one glorious moment in it all was your own First Communion day. We girls of the street could hardly wait as we rehearsed out our roles dreaming of that great day. But before it was merited you had to suffer the worst day ever, your First Confession. That was solemnly preceded by the trial of your life, the Catechism Test. We were tested at school, by a priest of the parish who made unheralded visits to each classroom in turn.

On his arrival, we all made a circle a few feet in from the walls of the room. He sat in the middle, black-frocked and grim, and darted questions backwards and forwards, in every direction, like the gone-wrong hands of the big Paper Clock, from which as baby infants we'd learnt to tell the time.

"Who made the World?" – "God"

"Who made God?" – "God"

"Who is God?" – "God is God the Father, God the son and God the Holy Ghost"

It made little sense to us, for we recited the answers sing-song. If one lot of words didn't do for the first question, they might for the next. It seemed more a case of just holding on in that circle of eyes. For eventually you knew every answer by heart. How easy it all was then!

To make matters worse, our family never seemed at ease with traditional ways. Someone ere long was sure to bring in their own odd approach. "Less of the Culchie", was how they looked at it.

At Confession Miss Sean took a line all his own, and he took it seriously as well. For weeks beforehand he collected up his sins, writing them out neatly in Your Ma's old cookery book, the one from the war that was needed no more.

He made us older ones pause: "Didn't you culchies divide yours into mortal, venial and reserved? I'm thinking, did you even know your sins at the time at all?" We were forever trying to steal Miss Sean's big book of sins to see inside it. We never succeeded. He took it with him to his first Confession, carrying it solemnly the whole way into the Confessional Box to read out.

The rest of us were ready and waiting, kneeling in position outside. He took quite a while to emerge.

"Sure, he only let me read the half of it," he told us, quite vexed. "He seemed to think I was taking the micky which in itself is a sin, so he said."

"What Penance did he give you?" we demanded in one voice.

That was the test, in our eyes an achievement to get anything more than the usual "three Hail Marys and say a prayer for me". We held in great awe anyone who managed more. Now Sean had a whole rosary to say.

Though as you grew older or got scruples you might well do that. Scruples was a curious disease, a troubled state of mind which seemed to inflict people out of the blue.

"Wee so and so's got the scruples," you'd overhear someone say of some young person they knew.

"Unsettled, wasting away, gone to skin and bones. Too in on themselves, you know, their conscience not now at rest." We knew very little in fact, than that those with it, stayed in Confessional Boxes longer, and when they came out the Penance stakes shot up. Looking back, we half-tried to catch the scruples ourselves by sitting close up by them, examining them carefully as in great mental agony they examined their consciences at Mass.

All told, you suffered a lot for your First Communion. You were summoned in early the evening before from your play and your hair stuffed with old newspapers for the making of ringlets. You dared not show your face again that evening, knowing you'd be the laughing stock of the entire street.

In my own case, things were worse still, as I was swathed in Miss Eilish's former Communion dress with its wee covered silken milky-white buttons.

"It's not fair," I remember at the time crying to

Your Ma. "All me friends have got a new dress. I'll be disgraced in front of the world, never live it down. And as for that veil, why, it's got beads on the wreath straight from a coffin. What's more, when you bite into them they coat all your teeth. Now some of my friends have ones in a ring that pop open and shut and shine brighter than these."

"But it's such a good veil," sighed my mother with a patience that must have been born of prayer. "Didn't I go myself the whole way to Belfast city for it?"

The placation, I remember well, was a pair of bought-for-me shoes. Hornpipes they were, white patent, not black like those worn by the girls who did Irish dancing.

The King and I made our Communion together but the most preparation he had to endure was an early bath. Joe's suit still fitted him, he refused to part with it, so the King had a bought one just for himself.

On the Communion Day morning, in a state of sanctifyng grace, the King and I stepped out together to go to the church. We shared a sponsor between us. He walked dignified and silent a few paces behind. From almost every house on the way came other First Communion children, the boys stiffly conscious in their first ever suits. We girls were already spying out the size of one another's white Communion bags, for the wreath and the veil were the least important accessories. The First Communion bag was all.

Usually made of the stuff of the dress, it had a band of silk or satin ribbon for a handle. This you wore on your arm. It dangled limp and unfilled, waiting for later. It rained money on your Communion day. In truth, to us children that really was what the great day was about. That bag was but a wee begging bowl disguised in fabric. The boys used their pockets.

With the Sacrament over and in a further state of grace, the fun really began. A lucky few were taken out to a café or the big hotel for their breakfast, but most of us returned back home for our own. You had fasted from sunset the day before.

Breakfast eaten, you set off in great style on your begging trip, officially known as "going to show off your dress". I'm not sure what the boys called it. Chaperoned by a group of older girls whose own Big Day had gone, your rounds began. They took the form of presenting you at every household remotely related to you in descending order of kinship, from your godparents down. Once arrived at their door you just stood, shy and silent, like a statue let out of the church for the day, while they fumbled coins of unknown worth into the bag and into the boys' top pockets. You nodded thanks silently, then, as soon as you could decently get away, you were off to the next. Later on, you might manage a wee smile or a word of thanks.

There were few money notes given out, though you might get a ten-shilling one from your godmother. You knew it straight off, for it made no noise as it slid into your bag. There was always the worry that it might in truth only be a Holy Picture folded up in disguise or a relic that had touched the garment of some saint, so you prayed hard.

Your rounds finished, you returned home like a queen, your escorts in tow, to count out the spoils.

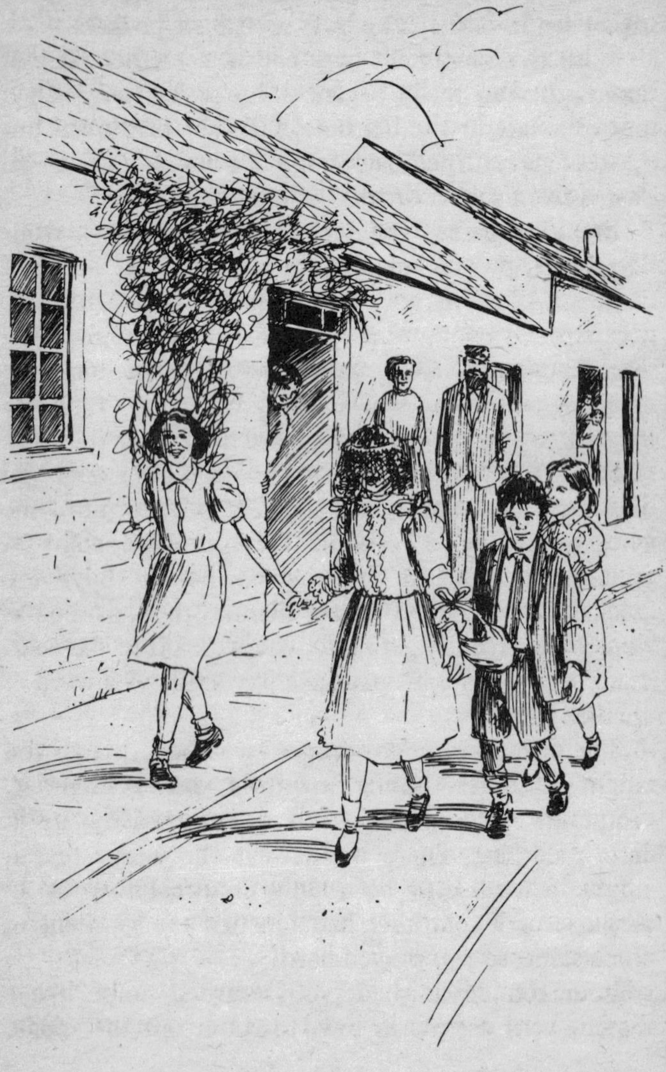

The bag was by now weighted down with many bright silver florins, heavier half-crowns, and the pink of that odd ten-shilling note. Here Your Ma intervened straightaway, taking some out to save for you for the next rainy day. With two pounds or so you were then given the freedom of the big shops down the town for what remained of the day and warned to keep well away from cheapjacks and the huxters.

Swanking it, you set off, linking arms with your best friend, a few lesser ones clutching on to your elbow, or crushing the life out of your veil. The most popular venue was the new modern Woolworth's and a big shop called Pennyworths which lived up to its name, Aladdin's caves to every one of us children. Here, every sort of toy dazzled you, paint-boxes and rainbow pencils, sets of crayons, whirly marbles, double-decker pencil cases made of bright plastic with, at the touch of a button, disappearing lids, wee dolls with sucking bottles, pink and white candyfloss, great mountains of sweets, some stuck fast. The hard black toffee bars, sandwiched with white, beloved by us all: the ones you needed a hammer to break.

Here was where one's gaggle of followers became increasingly vocal. Past debts were cleared, new ones entered into. With everyone licking up to you, and at every turn, new friends to be made, you were just dizzy with the power of it all.

Later on you kept bumping into the other communicant children, and you became aware of your dress, crushed now, and blemished with stains, and aware of your tangling ringlets in sad disarray. It was maybe the first time in your life you longed to have been born with a natural curl to your hair. But still, like all others, on your lips were those few breathless words, "How much did you get then?"

As the shops closed one by one, on the end of this day and a half, you returned slowly home, your pockets empty, your heart full, carrying your sweets and wee toys, and something somewhere for Your Ma that had been earlier wrapped up in style. Like the white dress now, it was sadly sticky and soiled. Your thoughts were now on your Confirmation day, when the whole lot would be played out again. But when that came round, being older, somehow it was not so much fun. Strangely, it was a holier day.

9

The church coloured our lives in many ways. One in particular was the keeping up with wakes. This was one of our street's most favourite games, best of all on a Hallowe'en night. When anyone in the neighbourhood died, in no time they called out the name at church and where the funeral procession would start. The family of the dead one took to wearing black cloth triangles on the arms of their coats as a mark of respect. Some used black-edged handkerchiefs. You watched them in church, which they now attended more often than before.

The last remains of the dead, as the body was called, were dressed at home as was the custom in those days. With a particular interest in the whole proceedings we would discover the street where the dead person had lived, praying hard that it would be far enough away from our own home for our faces not to be known. Finding the house itself was easy, as a black crêpe cross hung from the open door.

A group of us gathered outside, double-daring each other to slip in behind those others entering to offer their condolences and pay their last respects to the dead. In relays we'd creep upstairs to the wake room where the corpse was laid out cold, often on a real bed, a coffin with the lid off in readiness beside. The corpse would be all dressed up in its best Sunday clothes, hands joined, a rosary entwined through the fingers. Many wore brown scapulars on the neck, or were in a Holy Child shroud or Child of Mary habit if they'd belonged to those holy societies in their lifetime. All the rooms had that same faintly sweet smell of decayed apples.

A few old people would usually be settled in chairs round the walls, lamenting, and minding tales of the corpse's life. "Do you mind the time," they'd start off.

People would enter all the while, saying, "I'm sorry for your loss," and nodding, "it's a lovely corpse." Then they would sit down for a time to mind something themselves.

We would religiously cross ourselves, and fall to our knees to say a few wee prayers for the soul of the dead, our eyes on the bed to study the corpse, for it held a great fascination, that stillness of death. Our eyes would also be on our watches though, for the aim of the wakes game was the timing, who could clock up the longest time with the corpse. You knew you'd soon be seized with a fit of the giggles which would signal the end of your turn, and you'd have to make your way out.

In our family's case, we always prayed that Your

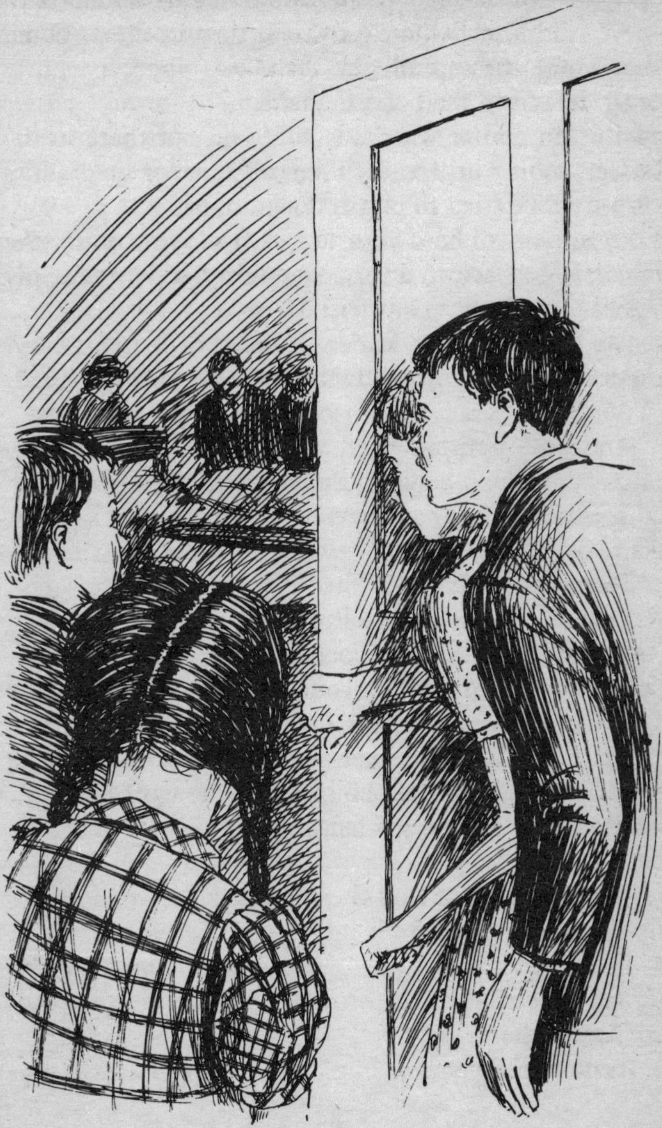

Da, dropping someone off, wouldn't be about. You never did know where he would turn up next. Often not home himself till the town was abed, he knew everyone from the policemen down.

But no matter what was going on out there in the street, sooner or later we'd be called in for the Family Rosary. We tried to play it down, outside.

"Can you all hold your horses, I'm away on for the Rosary, be back in a jiffy, so don't you dare take my place," we'd say to our friends.

As Joe was often leader, it worked just that way. "Are you looking for a fight?" he'd say slowly. "Fight Your Match then," and back you'd be in your place.

Indoors, too, we tried to play down the Family Rosary, make it a game. But to Your Ma it was much more than that. She believed it was prayer which kept families together. It was what kept the faith of our fathers alive in Ireland down through the years.

The Mysteries of the Rosary, as they were called, seemed joyful, glorious or sorrowful at will, untempered by any moods of your own. They changed by the day of the week and the week of the liturgical year. Even Your Ma had to refer to her book to get the right one. But her litanies she knew off by heart. Our Lady's Litany was her favourite:

Holy Mother of God
Mystical Rose
Tower of Ivory
House of Gold
Ark of the Covenant
Gate of Heaven

Morning Star
Queen assumed into Heaven . . .

The one of St Joseph came a close second.

Illustrious son of David
Splendour of Patriarchs
Mainstay of Families
Mirror of Patience
Glory of Family Life
Terror of Demons . . .

We'd murmur the words in chorus from behind the big couch, and from behind odd chairs. Each evening one or other of us was chosen to read out a bit of the day's litany. The others improvised the while.

Big Head most Pure
Big Head Divine
Big Head Most Courageous
Big Head Most Obedient
Big Head Most Powerful
Tower of Icecreams
House of Chips
Queen of the Culchies
Guardian of the Doc . . .

Your Ma would issue warnings that we'd have to repeat the whole lot again if we didn't attend. But often it got so out of hand, she couldn't maintain a straight face for herself.

Not all the families in the street were as holy as ours. Your Da often said it was because they ate chips.

The children of the unholy ones would be waiting without for you to come back to play, but if we'd had to resay the litany, then time itself was gone. The street would be deserted and you would be sent, with your guardian angel for company and no more about it, on up the stairs to bed.

10

Your Ma dreaded wet days with us all indoors on top of her. She was trapped between allowing us out in the rain to sail wee paper boats in the gutters, wet through, maybe catching double-pneumonia in clothes she'd be hard-pressed to dry, and making us stay indoors, the boys fighting mad with nothing to do but wreck the house. It took very little to become a regular ruction.

Such niceties as Miss were discarded. Like the Chinese we reverted to our animal names. Joe became "Horse", the King "Bull Runty", Miss Sean "Red Ned", Miss Malachy "The Gull", Miss Connor "The Rat". We girls, the "Three Mill Cats" – all saving Babynun, still under somebody's protection, who moved up merely a stage, to "Miss Babynun".

★ ★ ★

In no time it would be pure bedlam with everyone up to high doh in the chase. From one such row I can hear the cries even now.

"Miss Babynun, are you going to get it! Brother, you're for it, the Horse this time had gone clean mad; if you value your life, I'd run and run for it fast!"

"Where's that clever wee Rat and a half? He's getting far too cocksure of himself, wants a box on his ears, just wait till I catch him."

"That Bull Runty needs a kick up his big royal arse."

"You're not allowed to say that word, you big gulp."

"Bollocks."

"Nor that one either."

"I didn't."

"You did."

"That's a living lie – you're off your beano – talking daft."

Joe, the light of battle in his eyes, "Big Head, will you go to hell, but go backwards quietly so Your Ma doesn't hear. There's a good lad."

"Save your breath you to cool your porridge . . ."

A few went flying as they closed. Battling boys in every direction, even Miss Malachy in a temper at war with his looks. It was a row such as never before.

The three of us girls perched for safety on an upstairs window ledge with a pile of comic-cuts to hand, just looking on. There was an old wooden apple barrel on a landing upstairs, which had a lid with a ring on the top. For no reason now the three of us as one were bundled head over heels in, and rolled down

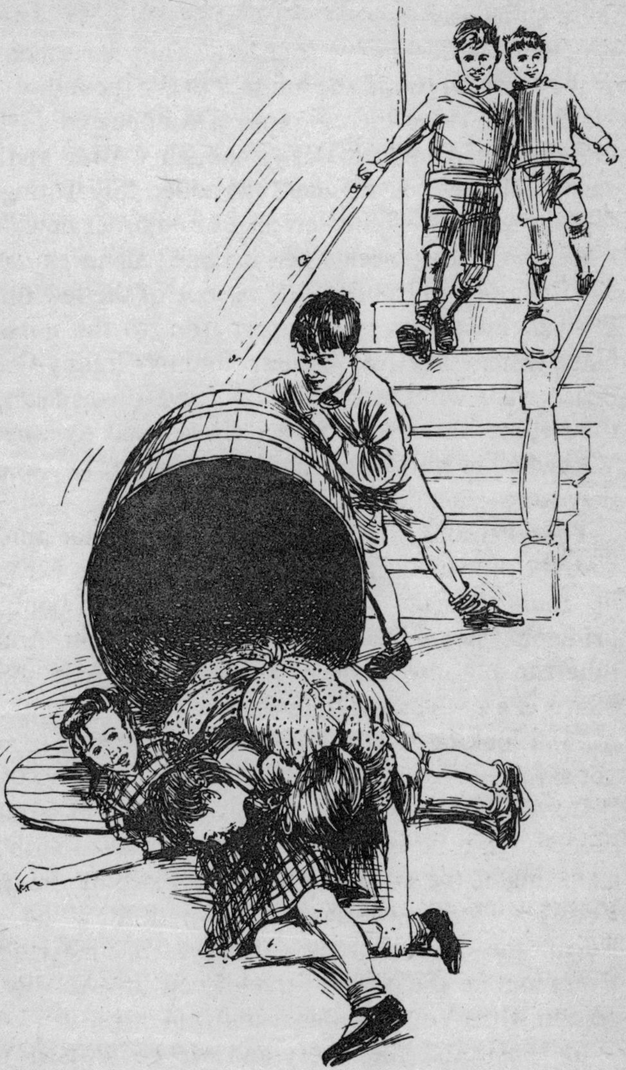

five flights of stairs to the bottom. It made quite a noise on its way.

"Holy Ructions, Blue Murder," Your Ma called it, as they tore on round the house, out for the kill.

"Hold it right there." Your Da appeared in the middle of it. One look wasn't enough. "Mind and be very careful of your tongues," he added threateningly. "Get some stock of yourselves, a bit of order now."

After one long week when it rained all seven days, Your Ma fled to Lourdes. It was one of the few times she had ever been away, apart from to the nursing home where she had babies. Granny-Granny-Grey-Beard went with her. Your Da drove them down to the airport, then rolled up his sleeves and took over. We had all to work much harder during the two weeks they were gone.

Your Da looked quite strange wearing her apron, with the pipe in his mouth. We lived on steak, because he could manage that. He bought it in pounds, bringing it home in a big parcel under his arm. And if time ran out, he made us drink raw eggs in milk. "Sure, it's all the same thing," he said, whipping them in, and looking slowly round to see if anyone dared not agree.

Lunchtimes were the worst, the house in strange silence. On a never to be forgotten occasion with us all sitting at the table, Fortescue in place by the fire, Your Da whipping away eggs into milk for all he was worth, the doorbell rang. That was the most odd. Everyone in the whole street knew it was closed session when Your Da was roaming at large.

Joe answered the door, and we could hear the

conversation in the hall. I can hear it now, almost word for word.

"Does Bronagh happen to be in?"

"Where else would she happen to be?"

"Might be out."

"Might be in, so why don't you come in yourself and see?"

It was one of Miss Bronagh's tripping of followers; she had them by the score. With a great show of gallantry, Joe opened the door. "Slide over," he told us, presenting a yellow-haired girl at the big open table. Everyone moved, no one spoke. I can see her now, blushing like a rose as she sat down. She looked shyly all about her in wonder, then fear, picking up Fortescue by the fire.

Your Da in his apron, the pipe in his mouth, glanced round. "What kept you? You're late. Will you take one egg or two? There's more whip in the two," he added slowly, already cracking them in. He came in from the kitchen and simply handed her the glass. "Get your teeth into that, that will keep the wheels turning . . . warm the cockles of your heart."

"You sup it," said Joe, still standing there.

"Here, wait a minute, you're not one of ours?" Your Da doing a rough count with his eyes, regarded her doubtfully. She shook her head silently. "No, I didn't think so. Where did you come into the picture?"

"I'm Mary-Jane," she said.

You could see Joe thought the name cute, not like us girls, one ailing and another harbouring a cough.

"That's a nice name," says Your Da. "You're not a Yank are you?"

She shook her head. "I'm called after my doll."

"May one ask which came first?" Joe inquired.

"It was my mammy's doll, it's still with her down in the South. I'm living with me auntie, just for my education – it's free up here," she enlarged.

Joe stared at her as if she'd committed an offence, the flicker of interest gone. The South to Joe was more and more the land of the culchies. A culchie under false colours she now was.

"With thinking like that you might as well be a Yank," says Your Da.

"I knew a Mary-Jane once," suddenly Fortescue announced. "She went to the dogs."

Everyone Fortescue knew seemed to have gone to the dogs at one stage or other.

"Sure, you don't know the half of it. A Gentleman of the Roads is that man sitting there, sober as a judge these days, not a suggestion. There's many a thing he keeps under his hat. Knew girls with names like Mary-Jane every day of his life. Isn't that right, Fortescue?" My Da was in full steam now. Even then he would have suited the stage, My Da.

"Aye, that I did," nods Fortescue, then, as if the effort of speech was all too much, he cleared his throat and spat right into the heart of Your Da's good fire.

Your Da shot him a look. "That's enough of that, Fortescue."

It was nothing to do with good health. It was considered an act of war to tamper with Your Da's fire.

"Well, wherever you're from," went on my father to the yellow-haired girl, "there's nothing of you. If I'd known you were coming I'd have cooked something else, for like one of the dying swans here you look like ye need fattening up. You'll eat a bowl of porridge, though, maybe, Goldilocks? I was saving it for the cat, but you can have it instead," he beamed at her now.

Beginning to turn up her nose, she stopped just in time.

"It's the medicine stikkin' out, just what the doctor ordered," Your Da dared her say else. Was he serious? To this day I don't know. By any reckoning he was a law unto himself, but he must have been aware of the fall of his words as Miss Joe must surely have known even then, he was a singular lad.

"You're not part of this patriot game, Mary-Jane – not for Ireland free – a nation once again, are you?" he now inquired slowly.

Whereupon I believe she said, "I was at the Cross and Passion Convent" or "with the Precious Blood Sisters beyond in Dublin." Something like that.

There was a dead pause in the proceedings.

"Are ye smart at your books? Do they give you slaps down there?" asks Miss Kilian to fill the gap.

Miss Sean took it up, "How do you stand on Ju-Jubes down yonder. As a true pillar of the church, I suppose you know your whole litanies in Irish then?" All of them became caught up in the game, if it was a game.

The girl took the best course she could, she simply sat there twisting round and round a lock of her bright hair. I can see her now, a startled look on her face as much as to say, "Better I'd have stayed in the South." Why her? Her only crime had been to ring a doorbell and hit Miss Joe in a contrary mood. And she was too new to the town to know that if Your Da's big dark cab was parked outside you didn't ring doorbells, you ran a mile.

The colour of beetroot, Miss Bronagh gave a stricken look at Joe, pleading for release before the porridge arrived. He took pity, maybe seeing the yellow-haired girl wasn't up to what he'd landed her in. He opened the door and stood politely to one side as Miss Bronagh and Mary-Jane fled tittering down the hall.

After lunchtimes like that and what went for food under Your Da's régime, we couldn't wait for Your Ma to come back. When she did, there was great excitement. Granny-Granny-Grey-Beard couldn't stop talking:

"Sure, they fed us on snails! Oh, you should have seen us!" she exclaimed. We listened in horror, our thoughts on the snails. We played the "snail game" outside, tapping them on their shells with a stone:

"Snail, snail, come out today and I'll give you a penny tomorrow," went the rhyme. The fat sluggy things would appear horns first, leaving a milky white trail behind them.

We felt sorry for Your Ma, thinking it was part of a penance she'd had to endure, but she confounded us further by saying indeed she'd really enjoyed them.

We all had new presents: Miss Eilish had a black doll, and I had a donkey with side baskets. Sadly, they became ornaments and were put away in the good front room. You'd see them at Christmas.

Everyone of us had new rosaries, fancy coloured beads, with the light shining through. We couldn't wait to get to the church, to use them. They came in an oval-shaped case like an egg, made of hard marbly plastic.

We loved rosary beads and would study them carefully, moving seats in the church, to get sight of a new pair. You could tell someone's standing by the rosaries they used. The religious themselves had sombre dark beads, often of wood, with a big wooden, no-nonsense cross at the end. Girls mostly had prettily coloured ones out of crystal, often fastened with medals, inlaid mother of pearl or Our Lady of Lourdes blue; enamelled and fashioned, they tinkled in passing. Boys had more nut-brown ones. Your Ma's were well-worn, she'd had them of old. She never did change them, but they often needed mending with the weight of medals and relics attached.

11

And the days and the years went on. Not much happened that wasn't the same. Something was always wrong with the cars, trees were in leaf or bare again, there were nights of no stars in the sky, and days of no rain, followed by ones when it would be lashing, you'd be trudging to and from school with your shoes letting it in. Some days stand out: riding dodgems in a trail of stars; slipping and sliding with the ground hard with frost; using roasting-tins for sleighs; long winter nights listening to the wireless, round the fire, and the memory of someone in the street getting lost.

As you grew older you played less in the street. You had to be intent on your studies, as your homework was now called and spend more time in your room slaving away at them. Later, we older ones gathered downstairs by the fire, until Your Da arrived in and banked it all down to keep it in touch for the morning. The bright merry fire would then be hissing with slack, its spirit all broken and gone. We resented this deeply the older we grew, after a full evening's studying, and often up later than him. But he never trusted one of us, not even Miss Joe, to bank the fire for him. One single look passed between father and son once on the matter. They faced each other, Joe by now taller than he; Joe told himself to lay off. To keep a fire going for a year and a day was one of Your Da's greatest ambitions.

The church remained a constant, as did the town's library. You could take yourself off to those any time, not needing permission. As such, I suppose, they were places well set up for use as excuses, but somehow one rarely strayed far from either of them. Bright lights were out. "They'll come soon enough," were Your Da's words on those.

The town's big cathedral was the same way as the library, you'd pop in and out on your way, just to say a wee prayer. The cathedral never was empty, there was always present a scattering of the seriously holy, lost in a humble mumble of private devotion, doing the Stations, making the Nine Fridays, the First Saturdays, keeping the Thirty Days Prayer and one we puzzled over in holy dread named the Perpetual Novena. Lone old women hands clasped high, heads bending up and down in prayer, counting the beads. There were even some young ones among them, praying to the heights with theirs.

The library was a popular meeting place. We often cycled there of an evening to change our books. The news spread like wildfire when new ones were in. Then there'd be a great dash from many directions.

We kept some in our family for ages. For as soon as one of us finished it, the other took it out. We'd never have dreamed of reading it collectively or anything like that. It had to be all officially stamped out by each of us. Other children at times chasing us, demanded, "When are you big bunch of smarties going to be finished with that there new book then?" We escaped often in a shower of stones.

It was round about this time that Joe acquired a new Bible. It was a strange old leatherbound book with the title St Elmo. It looked its age, dark, and not from the library, though none of us ever got near enough to make sure, not even to read for ourselves the author's name.

Now Joe could be seen, poring nightly over its pages, and was soon quoting from it. "I'll have to consider St Elmo's view on this," he began to say. In the coming days it was to become the main family refrain. When there was trouble about we now all took it up.

"I know, let us consult St Elmo straightaway," we would cry, playing for time. "I wonder what St Elmo would make of this shape of affairs, Joe, then?" But Joe soon was to work it in quite his own way.

On Wednesday afternoons after school there was a picture show in the boys' school, the fillums, they were called. It meant peace for a couple of hours straight for Your Ma. Those afternoons she traditionally set aside to make a ladylike little tea for us three girls, "To give you some feel for the finer things in life," so she said.

It was off with the boys' oilcloth and on with the

Belfast white linen, out with the good matching china, rimmed blue. Miss Bronagh did the flowers, Miss Eilish and I cut the sandwiches, laid out the table with the plates and a wee cake fork for each. Your Ma would have a cake complete with its icing, somewhere cooling. We'd have bought buns, too, delicately worked little pastries from the cake shop.

How we loved those names – Vienna Whirls, Madeleines, Cream Horns, Battenberg, but best of all after long years of trying ("I might and I mightn't . . .") we'd persuaded Your Ma to let us have bought chips. They were sold those days wrapped up in newspaper.

Those Wednesday chips were nothing short of conspiracy. As one of us ran off with the money to buy them Your Ma always warned, "Now, don't be seen carrying them. And whatever you do, don't let your father see you."

That was a relevant warning, for in the first case the chip shop was near the carstands, in the second, even if it wasn't, by the nature of Your Da's job, he could turn up there like a bad ha'penny anyhow. You learnt early in life to keep a steady eye out for his big black cab, for there was no knowing where it could loom next.

One Wednesday, I was back with the chips and we were just about to sit down to our ladylike little tea when the doorbell rang. Miss Bronagh went to answer it and the horror of it, in burst that whole mob of boys, early. The fillum had broken down.

Your Ma tried to run with the plates of chips to the oven. Miss Eilish had enough presence of mind to hide the plate of pastries under the table. And then they started:

"Oh ho, ho, ho. So this is what you do, when we're banished away," as one they cried.

Joe took over alone. "My, my, my, I thought chips were for the lower orders, the hard-reared, a sure sign of decadence, eaten only by wastrels, the down and outs, the criminally bent, ones who carry flick-knives, the half-bred in want of a good thrashing and less of them, the not-reared right. Here, King!" he cried, "how do you spell hypocrisy, boy? Miss Malachy! What's the Latin for chips? Miss Sean! Can you draw me a graph of a chip? Give the relevant equation. Young Connor! What would you say was the Catholic viewpoint on these here chips? Babynun! In your considered opinion what do you think would be Your Da's view on the matter? Oh, St Elmo, save me from hypocrites – for here is a house, and in this house here today stands a crowd of them, and one your own Ma," he finally cried, whipping in a sideswipe a handful of the offending articles. "If these ain't bought chips, Pardner, I never saw one."

Well, in no time, all was haywire. Our dainty little tea was set upon by that wild pack. It was an all-out raid, the oven emptied, under the table cleared, the lot demolished in seconds. "Well, I don't know," sighed Your Ma. "There's never a moment's peace the live-long day in this here family."

"It wasn't us made the fillum break down," Joe started up again, "it's those Culchie Holy Brothers." (That was a term of great abuse.) "Sure, they don't know their knees from their elbows. If you must send us to a school run by peasants." This referred to the fact that a lot of the town's Christian Brothers hailed from the South, which more and more to Joe was the land of Boglanders, if not by now the Culchie Headquarters. "They'd be better off with a plough in their hands, the half of them," on he went. "Did you see the Doc, Miss Connor, going at the projector like he'd stumbled happily into a turnip patch?"

This hurt our mother, who had a great respect for the religious, wherever they hailed from. She was a great friend of them all. She had her favourites, though. One of the masters at the Abbey Boys School she had a soft spot for was the said Brother O'Docherty – "the Doc" to generations of schoolboys.

We had one of the first television sets in our town, and we now saw a lot more of the Doc because of it. Our mother and he shared a common interest in Sergeant Bilko, the Yank army man who was on a lot in those days.

"Anyone at home?" you'd hear at the door and the Doc would step in. Then he and Your Ma would sit collapsed in a state of helpless giggles at Bilko's escapades. The funniest part of all was that we knew Your Ma really saw the Doc as an Irish Bilko. He certainly was a wheeler-dealer being a great hand at procuring tickets for All Ireland football finals when none were about, as well as holy relics, medals, Holy Water from Lourdes and other noted shrines. Holy anything from anywhere, you only had to ask and in the twinkling of an eye, the Doc could lay his hands on it.

Aside from Bilko, Miss Malachy only watched

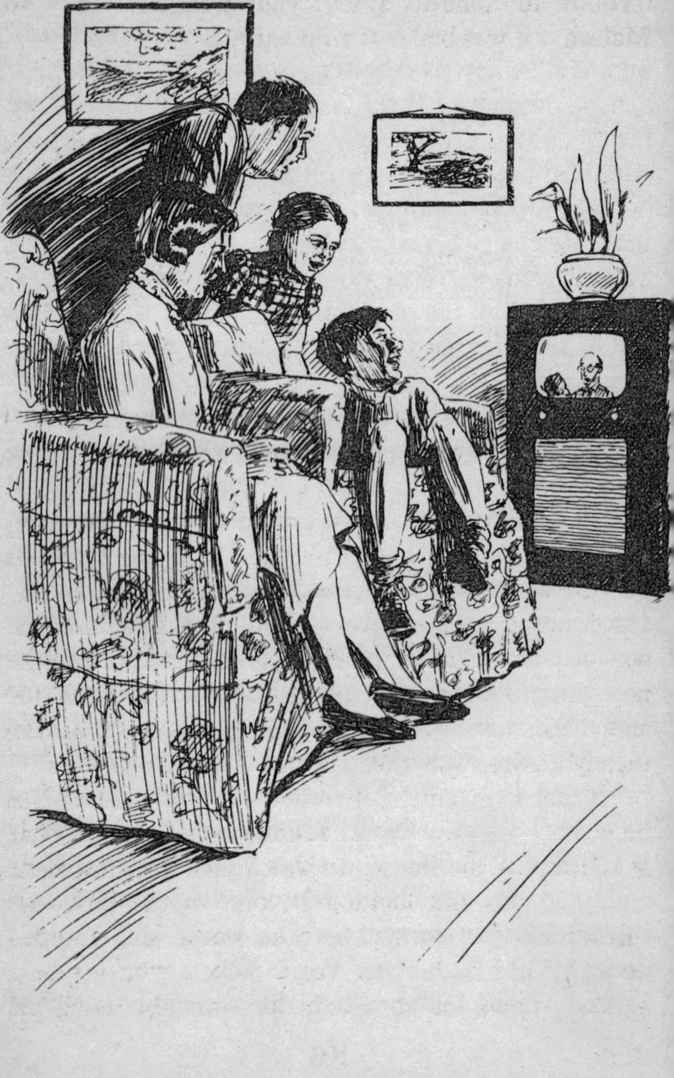

anything to do with trains and the weather. "Miss Mal," one of us would shout out to the street for him. "You're to come in quick, your weather's on." To Malachy, it was better than poetry.

> *Faroes, Fastnet, Irish Sea*
> *Rockhall, Shannon, Isle of Man*
> *Hebrides, German Bight . . .*
> *1001 falling . . .*
> *No icing in Iceland*
> *Winds variable*
> *Rain good, locally poor*
> *but rising . . .*

He'd intone as he listened. "Can't you culchies see – sure, it's as good as a litany," at the end he'd pronounce.

I suppose we must have grown to see it like him, for as I remember the weather and shipping forecasts became with Bilko a great favourite with us all.

I'm not sure how it came about, but soon the Doc was installed as official family tutor, which meant he now came almost every night. He tried to tutor Joe and me in Latin, and Miss Sean in maths, but even then Miss Sean was ahead of him.

"Is that Holy culchie Brother still down there? Has he gone?" Joe now would bellow at us from his eyrie at the top of the house. It was a nice back room he had, high up and looking beyond to the hills that surrounded the town. There he would sit, wrapped up in his old leather Air Force jacket, with maybe a blanket round his shoulders for warmth, doing his homework. His bible St Elmo beside him. "Jeez," he'd cry, "it's too much. How much can a man take? Haven't we the bloody Brother all day at school not now to be presented with him at night times too? What's Your Ma up to? no doubt feeding him buns, down there. Miss Malachy! What's the Latin for buns, boy? Miss Sean! Draw me a graph of a bun with the relevant equation. Here, King! Give us the Gaelic. Connor! Be a friend, will you? Go down there and get rid of him, tell him his school's had an emergency. It's on fire and he's wanted. I want me tay," his cries would echo from wall to wall.

Over the years, among ourselves, we'd built up our own culchie talk. It was, to our book, how the old country folk spoke. You had tay, your homework was doing your books, maths was telling your sums or counting your fingers and so it went on. Now we mixed it, switching like Joe, very often in the same sentence to a more precise Latinate voice, the type beloved by St Elmo, or so he assured us.

"Oh, St Elmo," you'd hear him cry, "what can a man do with the misfortune to be born into this here peasant land, to have nought about him but a bunch of culchies, whose very eyes can see no further than the nearest potato patch, whose very minds can give no thought to the higher things of life . . . who know nothing nor nothing care to know, as the line goes."

But eventually he'd calm down and emerge to go downstairs in his old Air Force jacket, rubbing his big nose as he went.

The Doc would jump up at his entry. Even the Doc was a little in awe of Miss Joe.

"Oh no, no, Brother, pray, pray, don't let me disturb you." Joe would stand there a moment. "Make yourself at home. Not that you need telling," he'd add under his breath. The Doc would relax further back into Your Da's special chair, watching the TV.

Love between man and woman, "High Romance" as we called it, was a buried story then, but if anything uncertain came up on the screen while the religious was ensconced in our midst, we had our own way of dealing with it. "Now what do you think St Elmo would make of that then, Miss Joe?" one of us would cry, or in chorus we'd chirp:

"Oh cheep, cheep, how big the world is," and lapse into nursery rhymes.

Often the Doc stayed for the family rosary, which, in view of his status, he led the whole way. With a professional in our midst, it was bereft of all sport; we answered deliberately, praying he'd make a mistake.

12

It was round the same time too that the King became head altar boy, and the doorbell rang more than ever. "The King's forgotten his soutane, his slippers, his surplice," or whatever it was. A messenger from the vestry would be posted outside, waiting to collect the forgotten article.

"Getting holy, I see, little brother," Joe growled at him. "make sure you ring those bells a bit earlier, boy, if you're on the first Mass tomorrow. Some of us have work to get on with. You might just study again the Departed Brothers line that ends the prayers at the Mass – yes, that's the one, if not . . ."

We'd troop to whichever Mass the King was serving, willing him with our eyes to spill the wine, drop the host, (we truly believed it would bleed), mix up the bells or whatever else could get him put in a state of disgrace. And each one of us would steadily avoid receiving the Eucharist from the priest the King was serving for, even when there was no queue involved. But the King went sailing on.

So much of all our lives, then, went on in the church. You prayed hard and there were graces and penances over the years. You met your friends there. They'd save you a seat. You did time like all others fancying the altar boys, led now by the King, looking debonair. You knew every line of their faces. The Mass helped with your Latin, for the priests spoke it then. Exercising your five senses, you felt at ease with the grandeur of the music, the colours, the incense, the forms. You'd live in the hope of a miracle unfolding before you: "Hey, you don't think, do you, that the statue of our Lady of Dolours has moved a wee bit?" you'd often whisper to your friends already squinting beside you.

You were at home with every sickness for no one was hidden away. You studied them all, wondering if they prayed, what they prayed for.

The whole town knelt there, every rank and fashion. There were the pillars of society, the matinée idols, the show-offs of the first class; ones killed with grandeur, the pippety-pips, the tricky pieces, the hard articles. The one who'd married a heretic came on her own, "He wasn't a Catholic you see – a solid Protestant but a good man in spite," it was said. There was the one who dressed like a heathen, and ones too in on themselves, the dance-goers, ones left on the shelves, ones flying their kite, the not married-right, the crosspatches, the strings of misery, bitter stop-the-clocks at any mirth, the granite-hearted, the giddy girls, the Holy Marys of men, too neat about the feet, it was held; ones hitting the bottle, ones soon on the road, ones about whom not too much was known, (Her in her high heels who wears the trousers though . . .). In among the good and kind, in an innocent sort of way, I suppose you saw it all.

You also inspected the fashions, remarking on styles, working your way through the poplins, seersucker and serge in their season, box pleats, gore pleats, accordion pleats, bias-cut lines to flare. At Easter, picture hats were in a class of their own, a sudden explosion of colour; buttercup yellow, lilac, plum colour and bright cherry red came up again and again. Everything about a costume matched from head to foot then.

Your Ma wasn't too taken with fashion, being more conscious of wear and tear. The three of us girls, our hair parted, sat there in crisp cotton dresses with names like Polly Flinders well into our teens.

In Lent just before Easter came the big parish retreat at which there would be visiting preachers, sometimes from afar. Like minstrels of old, some had great reputations – "He's a hard man that one, the J. from the South." – "He sure knows his stuff, if from a very odd order," was said of a Jesuit, a Redemptorist or such. We even once had our own dignitary from Rome, a local boy who'd made it all the way to the Vatican. His mother sat upright and proud in the church. He wasn't much cop back with his match. But he sounded grander in the Latin. "Should stick to it," people said.

Often we had missionary bishops in crimson-red robes, with an entourage of young black priests in attendance. These were very intent on our pocket money for their wee black babies.

The King at such times came into his own. "It's not easy, you culchies, to know what to do," he'd instruct us. "A bishop from Africa needs certain respects. There are special ways of addressing them that's demanded, as well as such things in this town tonight called bishop watchers, from the South, whatever that means." For the King as head altar boy, it was a tense time of year.

"It's just like the opera, hides a multitude of sins," was Your Da's verdict on the lot. He had driven the town's opera singers of old.

Your Da often drove the young missionary bishops as well. They stayed in the house of their order, far out of town. We girls couldn't credit he'd been in touch with such fame. Sure, the half of the school was crazy about them. We all had our fantasies of lonely missionary men, in need of loving helpers out in the field.

On the last few retreat evenings, which lasted a week, the big guns were brought out. "What we need is young men to join the toil in the field. Let us together now pray for vocations." The missionary bishops were the worst.

There was much confab and conscience amidst various families long after that week. A few boys joined up.

"It'd fit them better to have a gun in their hands and be out defending the Empire," was Joe's fixed belief, "than stuffing litanies into them who know better. Oh, St Elmo, save me from such holy ploughmen who have forsaken their own potato patch to travel afar digging for souls. Miss Connor! The Latin for potato, boy? Miss Sean! The relevant equation? Babynun! How do you spell anthropology, and when you look it up later, take note what it means," he cried.

But the holy women of the town, (the Greek Chorus, Joe called them), dabbing their eyes, shed tears of joy. "Wee so and so. Sure, have you not heard it? Has just joined the White Fathers, the Passionists . . . well, some sort of order."

It was never the Js; they didn't canvass; the Jesuits were too grand an order for that. "Sure, you could be a doctor twice over, before you were through with them," was the common belief. A cut above the others indeed were the Js.

The grand children of the town would be back home from distant boarding schools for the Easter holidays after the retreat. Like the Js they were a race quite apart. They strolled down the main street of town in the evenings, usually in uniform, casually tossing the scarves on their shoulders as they went. They only talked to each other and moved in a group. It was said they'd get wee things in their hair maybe, if they strayed anywhere else. Like the corner boys, it seemed they had lost the power in their elbows and wouldn't be seen dead now with a bucket in their hands. Out of uniform, they still looked the same: both the girls and boys in camel-hair coats. Your Ma thought these smart, and always remarked on "those nice camel-hair boys" when she saw them at Mass.

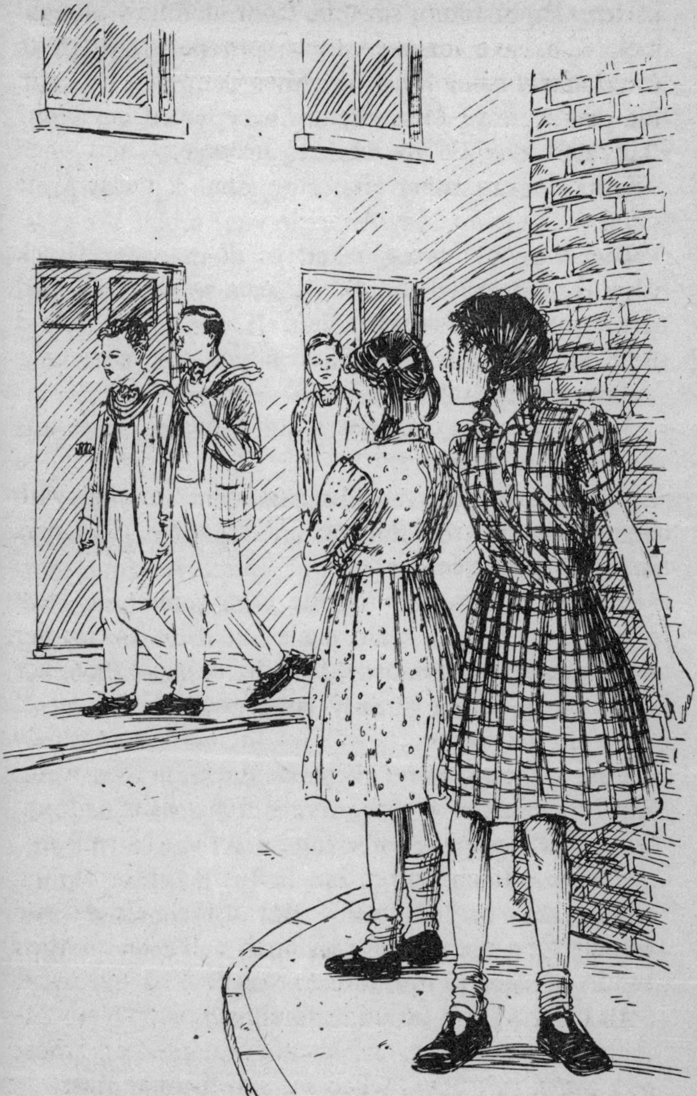

Their fathers were the big shots of the town, the doctors, bank managers, big shopkeepers, and that. You'd finally meet up with them at the university and find they were so definitely ordinary, you'd get quite a shock. It took a brave while to get over.

Then Lent, another Easter gone, and it was May again, the time for May Altars in your room. We girls remained loyal, having taken to them seriously as babies at infant school. We'd have to find, beg or borrow a Statue of Mary first. If you failed there, you'd have to make do with a picture, but then you couldn't make it "a nice wee veil" with its bright garland of flowers. There was quite a rivalry between us for the best one.

How innocent we were! I see us again, scouring the countryside for the flowers on our bikes, usually bluebells and primroses they were, if Your Ma couldn't be persuaded to part with something else from her plot. You could cycle out to Cissie Dash, whose garden was renowned for its unusual blooms, but often hers had already gone away to the local Carmelite convent.

"Oh, St Elmo, save, preserve me from idolators, these worshippers of pagan rites," Joe had his say. "Sure, that's where it hails from, don't you learn from your books? It's a load of old Ju-Ju, Bacchus, Odin, Diana, that sort of stuff." But we consoled one another, "It's just that he's jealous," and called, "Ma, would you listen to that son of yours!"

"Joe, that's terrible talk," she sighed.

Michelle Carrington

Loves

23070
5322
854

13

But it couldn't last. We were all growing up. Miss Eilish was the first to go. She went off to the Teachers' Training College in the city. Your Da drove her down, armed with a suitcase the size of a house and a big bag of sweets. With these she started out on life. But from nuns to nuns wasn't much of a change; in many ways it was a more sheltered existence. She grew fat from the stodgy food her first year, and fed us stories of girls and boys going to dances, all dressed up in white but for black stockings or the other way round.

The Beatnik era had arrived.

"Oh, St Elmo, grace us with your presence. Save us from these unknown harlequins and minstrels," cried Joe. But we listened very carefully.

The Doc continued his tutoring that winter, in between Sergeant Bilko and Your Ma's cooking. With Eilish gone, Joe and I grew closer that year. Often we sat in his eyrie at the top of the house discussing our homework and our future. The others piled on his bed, a willing audience. There with St Elmo and the Lone Star Ranger looking down, Joe would stand gazing out towards the hills and plan out all our futures.

"There's a big world out beyond there," he'd say pointing to the far distant hills.

"Cheep, cheep," the little ones would cry and cry.

"There must be more to life than this boghole, then," vexed, in the end, he'd say in the same restless voice.

But there was a quietness in his face. Looking at him, you knew then he would go. He was looking for a way out.

Joe was changing. There was now to be found more army information, battle plans and stations than ever tacked up on his walls. He was changing, and more lost in thought than before. Windy Hill now was rarely mentioned. He gave up his football and buried himself more and more in his books. He read poetry and Latin verse, staring out at the hills, wrapped in his greatcoat with his blanket on top.

The next year both he and I passed into the university, fed full of St Elmo and the Doc's Latin. We went up together. Once there, in many ways he vanished, led very much his own life. He joined the Army Corps, a very unusual thing for a good Northern Catholic boy. He now rarely came home at weekends, always being in training or army camp. Anything Irish seemed to become more and more of a penance. Most of his friends were from England or further.

Then he took to returning at weekends in his full OTC uniform.

"Oh, Mother of God, what did I do to deserve it?" cried Your Ma, "to have a son of mine in the British Army, so young."

We others used silently to wonder, would she mind, more, less, if he were to be older: Your Da was not to be told.

Joe studied Latin, Geology, Climatology, those sorts of subjects, in between his army training, so to speak. I drifted into my own way of life. We met very rarely – mostly at home.

Babynun now made more money than ever.

"Would you cut me a plug of Your Da's tobacco, Babynun," Joe would ask.

"Bac'ky Boy!" he'd roar, if Babynun stood hesitating, doubting this was allowed.

"Oh, St Elmo. Why stand I here . . . ? What indolence, what lack of grace have you bestowed on this here family," he'd sigh. "Which reminds me, how's your sums coming on, Miss Connor there? Still counting on your fingers are you, then?" But all that fell flat now. Connor was at big school, a keen footballer and trying to live up to or down, as the case was, his brothers' reputations.

The talk grew thinner and flatter. Soon the King arrived at the university, and in no time at all was sailing on, head lighting expert for the Drama Club, head of this, head of that. He studied law.

"Law, me lad," Joe had yelled at him, his first A-level year. "Law rooted in Latin is the future. Can't you learn from the conquering race? Leave English to the culchies. The interests of history apart, we won't mention, for where? the other: your few lines of Gaelic. 'In the ranks of death you will find them . . .' as the song says."

So Miss Kilian did law. His future had been sealed on the one word "satisfactory". "It was very satisfactory," he had written in some composition or other.

"Oh, St Elmo save us from peasants, the slow of mind," Joe had cried. "Where's your language? Don't you know your Eliot, boy? How can a thing be more or less satisfactory? It's an ultimate word, you eejit. But I don't expect the Doc and his like would know about that."

The King, in love with all things Irish, stood with round serious eyes, noted, thought it through, and did law. By that one word was his future sealed.

Joe played his last card, one spark of final glory before he left us. Miss Sean was to go up to the city for his university interview for the Faculty of Sums, as we termed it. It was his first time to the city and Joe for old times' sake agreed to meet him. For many, many days beforehand he bombarded Miss Sean with Ordnance maps, charts, campaign plans of where they were to meet. The poor child trailed half round the city, it seemed, seeking the rendezvous, rolling out very large maps as he went. He was finally picked up by the RUC, who looked at him and them with interest and would not believe he hadn't got his hands on classified documents somehow. He landed up in the police station.

Your Da had to be sent for. He drove down to retrieve him. Babynun had cycled to the carstands for him. "You're wanted home quick. Miss Sean's in gaol in the city," he was told. Your Da received the news without comment, but knocked out his pipe.

Things were changing fast. By the time Miss Sean and Miss Malachy reached the big "cheep cheep" world of the university, Miss Eilish had qualified as a teacher. Joe had taken a degree and gone away all alone to become a monk in New Zealand. It was just like him. He had chosen an enclosed, very feudal order. St Elmo would have approved. He left one summer's day. It seems a long, long time ago now.

Your Ma was a mixture of heartbreak and pride.

"Oh, what an order," the holy women of the town would tell her. "Do you know they can't talk, have taken a vow of silence, don't you see? And they have to rise at dawn, to dig a shovel full of their own graves, each and every day, I believe."

Something gave in her heart, I'm sure, the day he went away. The few letters that were allowed became more and more Latinate, but they seemed happy enough. He seemed to have found peace at last in his far-flung monastery.

Now the King reigned supreme. The next year, three of the boys overlapped at the university together, Miss Malachy following Joe's footsteps in time to become the first Catholic Chairman of the University Northern Unionists, his career coinciding with the new liberal Prime Minister, and fading out with him.

The King, waiting in the wings, was to take over as a leader for the other side with the People's Democracy.

Miss Sean vanished more and more into his own Einstein world with his sums.

Joe for a while tried to reinstate St Elmo and the Lone Star Ranger in his letters from New Zealand. "How are your sums coming on, Babynun?" he wrote in the latter's A-level year. "What's the Latin for Democracy, Miss Connor? Is the Doc one of them Democrats yet? Never forget, boy, St Elmo's an autocrat. It's his considered opinion, all these here new ideas might just be for the Culchies." But the tone grew thinner as he became more enclosed in his spiritual home far away.

All about, times were changing. Your Da's authority grew less. He still ruled the roost but the birds had flown. Miss Bronagh by now was a career girl. She had been the only one who'd made a stand on "stopping her studies" and gone to work early. "Work!" Joe had cried at the time. "Sure, that's for the culchies. Miss Connor, the Latin, boy?" – "Laboro, laborare, laboratum . . ."

Miss Bronagh became the chief confidant of Cissie Dash, who had become increasingly alarmed "with all them there books". "Sure, what's the use of it all? Where will it end? There's something amiss in the land," she was heard to remark.

Even Babynun was fast growing up. Miss Connor, with talent to spare, was becoming a hard man, as they say, a great raconteur with an eye for the girls. They were lads for the times and the times were changing.

Like others around, it was as if you'd turned your

back for a moment and they'd all grown up. Everywhere were boys and girls just a child's height but grown-up.

All about was change idling in the air, you could smell it. The Corner Boys even were afoot. Forsaking their walls, acquisitive of territory, ambitious of notice, they sauntered round town now, known as Teds. The nice camel-hair boys were often seen with them.

Miss Connor and Babynun were zealous in joining, increasingly looking like acceptable candidates. For them, careless of order, desirous of change, St Elmo was no more, he held no sway with them. He fled the land now, returning to Joe.

"What's up with the lot of you culchies over there in the North?" he now wrote. "St Elmo appears to have washed his hands of the lot of you. Bent on destruction, you'll draw the wrath of all Ireland on your heads. The culchies have won! It'll be chips everywhere . . ." He lapsed back into Latin if he wrote now at all. Brave words, foreshadowing the future in many ways. The storm clouds were gathering, the political scene having all but arrived.

I left to travel, see some of the world.

"What tidings from that wee lassie of yours?" the King overheard the neighbours ask of Your Ma.

"Oh, I believe she's reached the Middle East now," answered Your Ma, and with as much pride as wonder in her voice, reported the King.

Our mother got ill the next summer. "Oh, I'll be right as rain, in no time. The spring will see me better. It's just them ole mushrooms I ate," she wrote to say.

These she had recently tasted for the first time in her life, on a rare dinner out with Your Da. But it was more serious than that.

I made my way from abroad to see her.

Your Da sat by her bedside, they could do no more than hold each other's hand. I looked at him. Still that rock of strength unshakable down the years, but the doubt was there. His face told it. He feared the worst.

"Now that's what I call a nice pair of shoes," I remember her saying.

"They're Hush Puppies," I said, swallowing back the tears. I saw such a change in her. "I'll get you a pair when you're better, back to yourself." But I knew then it was not to be. She died within the month.

"Just worn out, the creature," said Cissie Dash.

Miss Eilish's fate was set. She came back from teaching in the city to take her place, but all tradition died with her.

St Elmo was far away. Your Ma had never lived to fulfil her dreams of seeing her eldest son again.

Cissie Dash did what she could. She came and cooked every market day, all Your Ma's best recipes for those that remained.

For a while Your Da became as a shadow. "Ach, it's awful hard," was the most I ever heard him say and his head slipped to his hands. And from being a man who had but about done his church duties up till then, he now took over in her footsteps.

He could be found, at all hours, kneeling where she had knelt in her favourite little church over by the bridge, the one of our Lenten escapades. How long, long ago that seems.

"A good woman if ever there was one. There'll never be another like her this side of the grave," was the Doc's epitaph.

It was in its way satisfactory.

POSTSCRIPT

My father died last year as I write. He chose a stylish day, All Souls, always to be remembered throughout the Christian world. He wasn't ill for long and never knew how ill he was, still the centre of all round him in the hospital till he stopped trying, at the end in great pain. I sat at his bedside a few days before he died; he talked of his brothers in death as he'd never in life, how much he thought of them all. And strangely in the form of the young ward nurse he thought the world of, was standing in front of him the only daughter of one of his brothers, in charge. Perhaps a circle had closed.

"Maybe I was too hard on you all," he said to me out of the blue, his eyes absorbed. "I should have hung up my hat long ago, given you your heads . . . Did it, I suppose, for the best."

"No, no, not at all." Swallowing hard, I tried to ease his mind. But looking back down those long years, though we have all travelled on, I'm not so sure that goes for the boys. At times amid constant laughter, it was hidden tears. It's too easy a way to see just one's own point of view. It can't have been easy for them, I suppose, educated far beyond their father, to be silenced by a single glance from him almost to the end. For a girl, a man's always a man – we have our own ways. Perhaps their mother died too soon.

Eilish was there with him the night he died. She came into the room. His voice was laboured as he struggled in pain; "Do you know what I'd really love is a cool, cool glass of porter," she heard him say. Fighting back the tears. "Would you like a Drink?" she asked, ready to dash to get him the moon if need be. He shook his head, sat right up in the bed looked at her, "You don't understand. I made a vow to your mother. Not a single drop of the stuff past my lips to my dying day . . ."

I won't say he lay back and died; but it was within the hour. Even in death master of himself, in his own way ever his own man.

We waked him at home in the old-fashioned way. A good few hundred passed through the house that night, town's folk, country folk, listening with tears in their eyes to some of the talk that called back those old wake games.

"They don't make them like that any more . . ."

"Aye, a great leader lost in him, the last and the best of them . . ."

All dying out now. Our day is passing . . . Gone forever the old stock. And not much around besides. "Not a bit of wonder the country's the way it was."

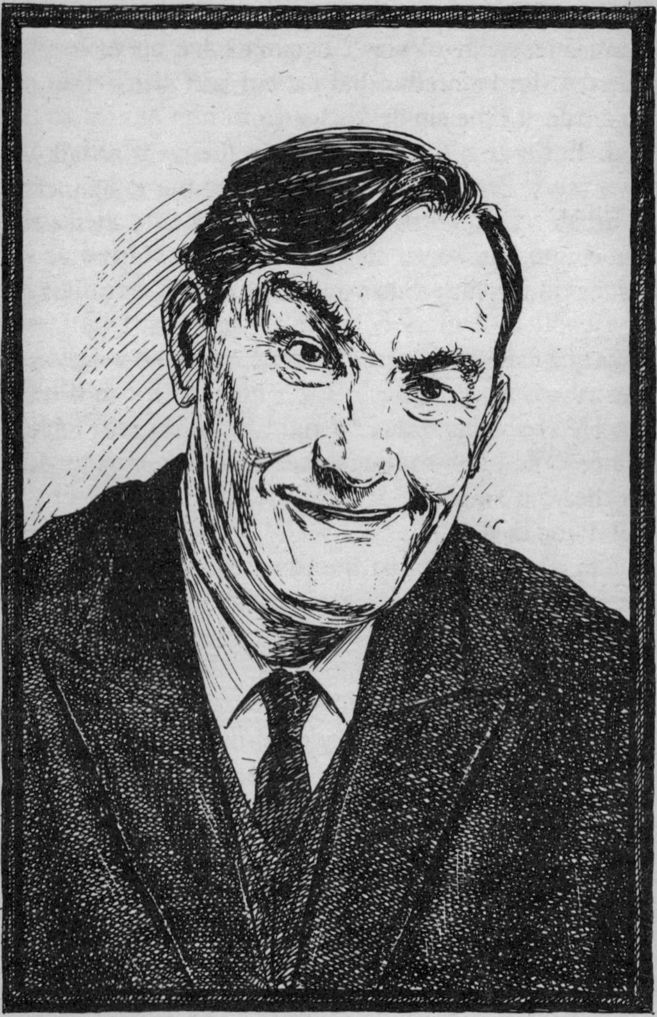

The morning after, Connor stood looking out of the back door. He shook his head slowly, moved the pipe in his mouth in an old familiar way. "Wouldn't you culchies just know Your Da's gone? A crate of empty spirit-bottles before me here stand and not a drop of milk even for the cat in the house."

The King in his position now in life went to talk to the army in charge in the town, to map out a funeral route taking in the old carstands, now in part sealed off. The army offered all they had, the soldiers stood to attention as his cortège passed; St Elmo would have approved.

They closed many shops and business premises for trading along the way, both sides of the sectarian divide. As one old garage hand said to Malachy of his lot's big brass, "Aye, they wouldn't for their own, but they did for Your Da, Mal."

He'd been above politics really, Your Da.

"There's no future in the past, in neither my time nor in your time," he used to say. "Get a hold on, build something of today. That's what'll last."

Five sons and the eldest grandson shouldered his coffin the last stage of the way. As Babynun said, "Now in this day and age that can't be bad."

Watching, it struck you then that Your Da wasn't tall – must never have been of any great height. No, not tall, just a big man.

When Marnie Was There
Joan G. Robinson

Brooding, lonely Anna, a foster-child, goes to stay with a kind Norfolk couple. There, like something in her memory, she finds the old house backing on to the creek. But it is the girl at the window who haunts her . . . Marnie, headstrong, often infuriating and somehow just as elusive when the two meet as she had been at the window. Marnie becomes Anna's perfect friend, and though she finally vanishes for good, she has helped Anna to make real friends.

This is a thrilling, intense story, part mystery, part adventure, part fantasy, and will appeal particularly to girls of eleven and upwards.

Harriet the Spy

Louise Fitzhugh

Harriet the Spy has a secret notebook, which she fills with utterly honest jottings about her parents, her friends and her neighbours. This, she feels sure, will prepare her for her career as a famous writer. Every day on her spy route, she scrutinizes, observes and notes down anything of interest to her:

> Laura Peters is thinner and uglier. I think she could do with some braces on her teeth.

> Once I thought I wanted to be Franca. But she's so dull, if I was her I couldn't stand myself, I guess it's not money that makes people dull. I better find out because I might be it.

> If Marion Hawthorne doesn't watch out she's going to grow up into a lady Hitler.

But Harriet commits the unforgivable for a spy – she is unmasked. When her notebook is found by her school friends, their anger and retaliation and Harriet's unexpected responses explode in an hilarious and often touching way.

'Harriet M. Welsch is one of the meatiest heroines in modern juvenile literature. This novel is a *tour de force*.'
Library Journal

All these books are available at your local bookshop or newsagent, or can be ordered from the publishers.

To order direct from the publishers just tick the titles you want and fill in the form below:

Name _____

Address _____

_____

Send to: Collins Children's Cash Sales
 PO Box 11
 Falmouth
 Cornwall
 TR10 9EN

Please enclose a cheque or postal order or debit my Visa/Access –

 Credit card no:

 Expiry date:

 Signature:

– to the value of the cover price plus:

UK: 60p for the first book, 25p for the second book, plus 15p per copy for each additional book ordered to a maximum charge of £1.90.

BFPO: 60p for the first book, 25p for the second book, plus 15p per copy for the next 7 books, thereafter 9p per book.

Overseas and Eire: £1.25 for the first book, 75p for the second book. Thereafter 28p per book.

Lions reserve the right to show new retail prices on covers which may differ from those previously advertised in the text or elsewhere.

Lions